Irish Railways
The Last 60 Years

MICHAEL H. C. BAKER

WORLD RAILWAYS SERIES, VOLUME 4

To my dear friend, Father Michael Murphy of Cobh and Cork

Acknowledgments

I owe much gratitude, as we all do, to the many members of the Irish Railway Record Society and the Railway Preservation Society of Ireland for all they have done in the 32 Counties, both jointly and separately, to keep a detailed account of the rich history of the Irish railway scene and preserve so much of it, from the most detailed paperwork and minuscule artefacts to no less than three of the glorious Great Northern Railway express engine 4-4-0s still in working order. Amongst the names to whom I am personally grateful are Brian D'Arcy Patterson, who made me welcome each year in his office at Islandbridge, Tim Moriarty and Gerry Beesley, and, especially Ciaran Cooney, who has been kind enough to check the proofs. Of course, any mistakes and inaccuracies are my responsibility alone. And finally, to Maeve, whose parents had the amazingly good sense to name her after Ireland's most famous steam engine.

Published by Key Books
An imprint of Key Publishing Ltd
PO Box 100
Stamford
Lincs PE19 1XQ

www.keypublishing.com

The right of Michael H. C. Baker to be identified as the author of this book has been asserted in accordance with the Copyright, Designs and Patents Act 1988 Sections 77 and 78.

Copyright © Michael H. C. Baker, 2021

ISBN 978 1 80282 164 2

All rights reserved. Reproduction in whole or in part in any form whatsoever or by any means is strictly prohibited without the prior permission of the Publisher.

Typeset by SJmagic DESIGN SERVICES, India.

Introduction

Travels around the Island of Ireland

Where to begin? To do it geographically seems logical enough. We could have done it chronologically or maybe alphabetically or perhaps we could have first looked at all those now vanished lines, stations and whatever else was left over from the steam age that was dependent on a pair of parallel lines to go about its business. We could have ended with those that have since appeared, which is a great more than one might have originally thought. But we are getting a bit abstruse, so geographical it is.

It was an early September morning in 1959 when I first set foot on Irish soil. I had travelled on the evening boat train from Paddington, Castle-hauled all the way, and had managed to sleep, off and on, during the three-and-a-half-hour journey across the Irish Sea, docking at Rosslare as a misty dawn broke. Ah, the soft gentle rain of Ireland, with which I would become so familiar once I had married Maeve in Dublin nine years later and she would regale me of reminiscences of her school days, with no great relish, in Connemara, where the aforementioned soft, gentle rain was the norm.

I had decided for various reasons to visit Ireland, primarily, I guess, because its culture interested me; it had so many links with ours but was still its own. I had a holiday job as a porter/carriage cleaner at Kings Cross station in London and got to know another student there, from Trinity College, Dublin, and he used to lend me his *Irish Times*, which I found to be the most literate and fascinating daily paper I had ever come across. That got me reading Irish authors, of which I began to think there must be an endless supply, and this turned out to be true, some of whom even had 'proper' jobs on the railways.

And then there were the railways themselves. They, too, were almost but not quite like an extension of our own. The five-coach train I boarded at Rosslare was painted green – well, it was Irish. Internally, its appointments were reminiscent of both London, Midland and Scottish Railway (LMS) Stanier and British Rail (BR) Mark 1s, whilst motive power was a Co-Co diesel. None of this surprised me; I knew that steam was rapidly being phased out and diesel was the norm as far as passenger working was concerned.

I spent the day in Waterford, the highlight of which was watching, and photographing in brilliant sunshine, the departure of the New Ross and Macmine Junction branch line train, which was composed of a clerestory corridor carriage dating from Edwardian times, and one of the curious Bulleid 'tin vans' four wheel, unpainted and a typical example of Bulleid eccentricity (I mean who else could have considered a four-wheel van ideal for passenger trains in the 1950s), hauled by a steam engine, No 159. This was a J15, otherwise known as a 101, the Irish equivalent of the LMS Stanier Class 5 in that it was the most numerous class of steam locomotive in Ireland and would last to the very end of steam. Two have been preserved.

Between 1866 and 1903, 111 J15 0-6-0s were built by Great Southern and Western Railway (GS&WR). Although scrapping had begun long ago, in 1885 to be precise, the J15s had established such a niche, even deep into dieselisation, that there would still be 53 on Córas Iompair Éireann's (CIÉ) books on my next visit to Ireland in 1961. There is a parallel here with the London, Brighton and South Coast Terriers. The span of the withdrawal dates of the class, 78 years, is extraordinary by any standards. Inevitably, many modifications were carried out in the 97 years that the class served the GS&WR, the Great Southern Railways (GSR), and CIÉ. Indeed, to quote J J Johnston, the one-time Assistant Mechanical Engineer (Technical) of CIÉ, 'the original conception and "bones" still remained throughout'. Some might compare the J15s to the broom, which during its career was fitted with three handles and four brushes.

That 1961 journey from Waterford to Macmine Junction was my one and only behind a J15, at least until the preservation era, but I did come across members of the class in charge of seaside specials

of six-wheel carriages from Cork to Youghal, and various goods and shunting duties, also at Cork and elsewhere. Although the design of the J15s is attributed to Alexander McDonnell, who had been appointed to take charge in 1864, the work was actually carried out by Charles Beyer of Manchester (Beyer Peacock would build many Irish locomotives). The 0-6-0 was, by general consent, the ideal wheel arrangement for goods haulage, not just in Ireland and Britain, but in much of the Continent, and would remain so into the 20th century. Although eight coupled locomotives would take on the heaviest duties in the 20th century in the UK, the only eight coupled GS&WR examples were a pair of short lived 4-8-0Ts. Some 2-6-0s also featured, but, for many freight duties, the 0-6-0 was never displaced as long as steam was king.

Right from the start the J15, with its driving wheels of 5ft 1½in, proved itself capable of passenger work and this, no doubt, contributed to its longevity, being perfectly suited to monopolising the many branch lines that the remoter parts of Ireland were endowed with, but which were fast disappearing by 1959.

On obtaining its freedom from Britain, financial penalties were imposed and Eire, as the independent 26 Counties were now to be known, found itself financially impoverished and the railways, like the country generally, had to be very sparing in investing its limited resources. A number of lines were singled, the furnishings of the few new carriages, which were totally in the GSWR tradition, were a little sparser than their predecessors, whilst new locomotives were few and far between. Edward A A Watson had been appointed as Chief Mechanical Engineer (CME) during World War One, having come from Swindon, and immediately set about what he fondly hoped would be an improved Star, with touches of the best features of the London and North Western Railway (LNWR) Claughton. These predecessors of the 800s were a class of ten four-cylinder 4-6-0s, the 400s. They were built between 1916 and 1923, four at Inchicore Works, and the others by Armstrong Whitworth. Sadly, Watson's hopes – he was apparently a tricky customer to deal with, and not much liked – were not fulfilled. Various faults, grave ones, began to emerge, and Watson took up work back in England. His successor, John Bazin, had to act quickly. He introduced three mixed traffic 4-6-0s, the 500 class, which proved to be excellent locomotives, and so various modifications, some more expensive than the others, were carried out on the 400s. Despite this, three were broken up in 1929–30, which, given the GSR's financial straits, was nothing short of a disaster. The surviving seven served well enough, being taken out of service between 1955 and 1961.

Undaunted, by the mid-1930s, Inchicore deemed that it was time to have another go at producing a 4-6-0 capable of hauling the heaviest and fastest expresses on the Dublin to Cork main line, and also able to tackle the ferocious 1 in 60 climb out of Cork unaided. Thus in April 1939, No 800 was unveiled and set to work. As a general rule, neither GS&WR or GSR went in for names, but No 800 and its two sisters were meant to be something special – and they were. No 800 was not only given the name of a legendary Irish queen, but the script on the nameplate was the Gaelic version, *Maedb* (*Maeve*). It was a truly impressive machine. Painted deep green with yellow lining, its designer, E C Bredin, in a message to the crews who would work it, declared 'a good deal of expense and trouble has been undertaken to give these engines an attractive appearance', and urged them to mind the paintwork. There are plenty of handsome locomotive designs which only flattered to deceive but No 800 and its two sisters proved to be all that could have been hoped for. O S Nock, probably the greatest authority on locomotive performance, came over from Britain for a run behind *Maedb*, to which he gave a rave notice; on one journey it attained 95mph, on another it lifted 17 bogies out of Cork, unaided. *Maedb* bore a striking resemblance to the rebuilt Royal Scots, particularly as it had a double chimney, a first for Ireland, but as it appeared several years before the first modified Scot, it was actually the LMS engines which resembled the Irish ones.

Inchicore was well aware of developments in Europe, particularly the work of the great Chapelon in France. Richard Maunsell, once of the GS&WR and the Southern Railway CME from 1923, was well thought of in Ireland, not least on account of the Woolwich Moguls, designed by him for the South

Eastern and Chatham Railway (SE&CR) but taken up by the UK government in the war. Twenty of them came to Ireland and worked Dublin to Galway, Cork to Rosslare and some Dublin to Cork trains. Following his retirement from the Southern Railway in 1937, Maunsell paid a visit to Inchicore and it is generally thought that his comments on the design of the 800s were noted and acted upon.

The second 800, No 801, *Macha*, entered service in November 1939; the third No 802, *Tailtiu*, in June 1940. By the latter date, World War Two was well under way. Eire was, of course, neutral but was affected in many ways. Many of its citizens took part, coming to Britain's aid, particularly if they had relations in the UK. Although others, who perhaps had been involved as young men and women in the fight for independence, whilst opposed to all that the Nazis stood for, saw the war as nothing to do with them. There is a story, probably apocryphal, told of a totally Irish Lancaster bomber crew, and there certainly were some trying to avoid the flak over Hamburg; the captain turns to the co-pilot and says, 'Thank God de Valera [the Irish prime minister] has kept us out of this'. Readers may know Yeats' poem of World War One, 'An Irish Airman Foresees His Death'.

The greatest effect of the war, as felt by the railways, was a drastic shortage of coal. Welsh coal had always been preferred but now shipping was dangerous, and the supply was so drastically cut that adherence to schedules became impossible, and there were examples of journeys, which once would have taken a few hours, being extended over days. This meant that the glory days of the 800s were over almost before they had begun. After the war, there were still shortages of coal. CIÉ introduced AEC/Park Royal diesel railcars in 1952, and the A Class Metro Vickers, Crossley-engined diesel electric locomotives in 1955, and really, from then on, there was no need for powerful steam locomotives. Nevertheless, *Maedb* became almost legendary; far and away the most powerful and perhaps the most handsome steam locomotive to run in Ireland. It could have given the LMS-rebuilt Royal Scots and the GWR Kings a run for their money, if only the gauge difference had not intervened. The GSR and CIÉ were immensely proud of it, and it featured in many publications and, although the authorities in the Republic, as Eire had now become, showed little interest in conserving railway heritage, scrapping

Plenty of freight business in evidence at Waterford in September 1959, as No 263 gets a grip on a lengthy Rosslare-bound mixed goods train. This 0-6-0 was one of a class of seven powerful locomotives built in 1914 to the design of R E L Maunsell, shortly before he crossed the Irish Sea to take charge of locomotive matters at the Ashford works of SE&CR, and, from 1923, of the Southern Railway. No 263 was withdrawn in 1962.

would have been unthinkable. Today, it is preserved in the Transport Museum, at Cultra, near Belfast. Pity a place could not have been found in Dublin, where it belongs but, of course, we are grateful, not for the first time, for the North coming to the rescue.

On my 1959 visit to Ireland, I had the good luck to come across one of the 400 Class 4-6-0s, which were all scheduled for withdrawal, at work, hauling the heavy overnight Dublin goods. Two years later, on 2 August 1961, my luck was even greater for on Cork shed, I found none other No 801, which was being readied for departure to Thurles. Some authorities claim it was withdrawn in 1957. It clearly was not, although No 802 had been and No 800 was semi-retired. I positioned myself on the Dublin side of the tunnel, out of which eastbound trains have to climb, and out it duly burst, in as immaculate condition as would have cheered the spirit of Bredin. Its load was far from what it had been designed been for; no 17 bogies here, instead a mere half dozen freight wagons, a sad end for a very special locomotive.

I once asked J J Johnston, who had been much involved in the design of the 800s, why they did not go the whole way and introduce Ireland's first Pacific. 'Because a 4-6-0 could do all we wanted,' was the answer. And, of course, he was quite right. Which leads to another question. Why bother with a 4-6-0 at all? The 400s, 500s and 800s were so heavy that they could not work off the Dublin to Cork line, other than the branch from Mallow to Killarney. All were seriously under employed; they spent a good deal of time either undergoing repairs or awaiting attention; not all the trains they normally worked really needed such power, whilst the delay caused in detaching the pilot after the climb out of Cork was hardly significant. Great Northern Railway (GNR) found the 4-4-0 could answer its needs, right until the end of steam, the post-war VS Class being the very last new design of 4-4-0 anywhere in the world. The 800s were very expensive to build and probably never recovered their costs – No 802 lasted just 15 years. The GS&WR had one very fine modern 4-4-0, No 341 *Sir William Goulding*, begun by Robert Coey and completed by Maunsell, and put into service in 1913. By all accounts it was an excellent engine, popular with the locomotive crews that worked it, and named after the chairman of the company, who surely would not have wanted to be associated with a nonentity. It was gone by 1928, however, despite being considered a better engine than those of Watson's 4-6-0s in their original condition. To quote Jeremy Clements and Michael McMahon in their definitive *Locomotives of the GSR*: 'The scrapping of this locomotive raised adverse comment amongst observers as being unreasonably premature for such a useful and competent machine.'

The GS&WR and GSR 4-6-0s were handsome, useful engines, but were they really best suited to the needs of the operating authorities? This is a question with more than one answer. Perhaps *Maedb* and its two sisters were, essentially, a vanity project, though one of the highest order, to be sure.

GNR of Ireland took a different route, partly, it has to be said, because there was not sufficient space in Dundalk Works to accommodate anything larger than a large 4-4-0. Their 4-4-0s were all Dundalk designed, although the great majority were built by Beyer Peacock. Distinctive, clearly family related and definitely Irish, even if there were hints of the long vanished English Great Northern. When I finally reached Dublin on 8 September 1959, after hitchhiking around the south and west, my first sight of a VS 4-4-0, No 58 *Lagan*, in its striking, well-polished, nicely lined blue livery, reminiscent of the Caledonian Railway, setting off from Amiens Street in charge of a long rake of brown painted carriages, similar to LNER, was something to behold. Bright blue engines and varnished mahogany carriages operating main line traffic within the British Isles; had I gone back in time, was this really 1959? I, of course, through magazines and books, knew what to expect of the company, which operated across the border between the 26 and 6 Counties, but perhaps I had never quite believed it. The three-cylinder VSs were the post-war development of the V Class Compounds of 1932. The latter had originally been painted black but, from 1936, were adorned in that wonderful blue livery, which can be seen on the preserved *Merlin* to this day. For a brief period, the V Class-hauled 15.15 Dublin to Belfast achieved the first mile a minute run in Ireland, between Dublin and Dundalk.

Actually, the GNR had disappeared in 1958. Declining receipts, road competition and a floundering management had seen it go bankrupt; its assets divided between the governments of the 6 and 26 Counties. Whilst *Lagan* still carried traditional livery, its GN initials had disappeared from the tender and the initials UTA (Ulster Transport Authority) were stencilled on buffer beams instead.

My intention on that first visit was to hitchhike as much as possible but also, where funds permitted, take the train, which was how I arrived in Killarney one Saturday afternoon. Killarney is like nowhere else in the island of Ireland. It is the gateway to some of the most beautiful and remote areas of the far west, and it takes the tourist business very, very seriously. GS&WR built a luxurious hotel there and Great Western Railway (GWR) offered what they called weekend excursions, by way of Fishguard and Rosslare which, apart from anything else, involved a lot of travel by ship and train, leaving Paddington on a Friday evening and returning on the Monday morning.

No sooner had I alighted when I was approached, as were other passengers, by touts for the various guest houses – I was clearly not of the class of clientele likely to patronise the Great Southern Hotel! The main street bore a striking resemblance to those adjoining the golden mile at Blackpool – except for the horses. They were everywhere, in charge of various vehicles with a capacity ranging from two to a full compartment. Their owners were desperate to persuade the tourists, especially American ones, that this was still the normal method of transport in the Emerald Isle, despite the presence of vast numbers of tractors, VW Beetles, quite a lot of Morris Minors and Leyland PS3 Tiger buses; although, admittedly, there were plenty of donkey and horse-propelled carts outside creameries. I have revisited

Killarney several times since, and in some ways, it is totally unchanged, although the trains in the station are more likely to be of Spanish or Japanese manufacture, rather than British or American. There is still nowhere quite like it in Ireland, which is probably just as well.

Next came Limerick, which was a busy transport hub – although that probably was not the term then in use – and a hot bed of Chicago-style gangsterism, of which the visitor was completely unaware. My future mother-in-law came from Foynes, and Limerick was the nearest big city but she never had much time for it. I found it an interesting city, not least because, despite being far inland, it was a busy port, on the River Shannon which, as I used to drum into my pupils, is longer than any other river in Ireland, Scotland, Wales or England. I also came across two intact, but about to be broken up, 4-4-0s, virtually the only ex-GSR ones with which I became acquainted; I never saw one working and none has been preserved. A great contrast with the GNR, of which there are no fewer than three, all preserved in working order.

From Limerick, I hitchhiked to Galway, the last calling point for Christopher Columbus before heading out across the Atlantic in 1492 and where, it is asserted, he took on one of its citizens as a member of his crew. It was and is an ancient, fascinating, lively city, a very culturally aware one, and the birthplace of James Joyce's wife, Nora Barnacle. On 7 September, I came across an ancient, but still much valued by the cognoscente, steam locomotive, to wit No 653. This belonged to a Midland Great Western Railway (MGWR) class of 2-4-0s, dating from the 1890s and, apart from one destroyed in the Irish Civil War, was very long lived, withdrawal beginning only in 1954. No 653 would work until 1963, the very last active 2-4-0 in the British Isles.

Various friendly drivers gave me lifts through the flat lands of the Midlands – at least one in the inevitable VW Beetle, a priest on the outskirts of Athlone, asked where I was from and wished me well, and so on a sunny afternoon I at last arrived in Dublin, a city with which I was destined to become more familiar than I could ever have imagined. Dublin had three main line stations: Kingsbridge, out along the Quays and beside the Guinness brewery, possessor of the most magnificent railway building in all 32 Counties; Amiens Street, which was really two stations in one, like London's Victoria; and Westland Row.

Kingsbridge flattered to deceive, for the interior did not live up to the promise of its splendid façade. It possessed only two platforms, one for departures, one for arrivals, with a shorter one let into the departure one. Between up and down platforms were several carriage sidings. If I had hoped to come across locomotives and carriages from long ago, Kingsbridge took me further back than any rolling stock, for its unaltered design was that of station layouts from the beginning of railways; Euston of 1837 being the example which springs instantly to mind. Euston, of course, grew and grew and eventually was totally rebuilt in the 1960s, losing in the process its iconic ceremonial arch. However, Kingsbridge, which connected Dublin with the south, notably Cork, hardly grew. There was practically no suburban traffic, as Kingsbridge was a fair way out from the city centre. Kingsbridge, renamed Heuston in 1966, eventually did its best to emulate Euston, along with sounding almost the same. Euston, of course, was where one caught the boat train for Holyhead and where so many thousand Irishmen and women first set foot on English soil. By the 1970s, Dublin city had grown enormously, 'commuting' had entered Dubliners'

Muine Bheag, County Carlow, is one of the finest country stations in all of Ireland. Dating from 1848, it is beautifully proportioned in the classical style and, as one can see by the window boxes, the curtains and the general air of well-being, it is greatly cared for. On the main line from Dublin to Waterford, it was actually closed in 1966 but was re-opened and staffed in 1988. I used to meet Brian D'Arcy, of the Rail Control Office, each summer in the 1970s at his Islandbridge office, midway between Heuston station and Inchicore Works. He told me more than once how much he regretted that ill-thought financial considerations had meant that so many smaller stations had lost their staff. An unstaffed station did nothing to boost passengers' sense of security, and even if relatively few trains called, the presence of staff who took pride in looking after their station was a price well worth paying.

vocabulary, and long-distance services had expanded. Heuston numbered nine platforms. At the same time, it had the good sense to retain its magnificent exterior whilst utterly transforming its rather gloomy interior. I never saw a steam engine at Kingsbridge/Heuston, not even in preservation days.

Westland Row was the only Dublin station that had an arched roof, which gave it a certain presence. It, too, had only two main platforms, but it was not a terminus in the proper sense of the word. Although it did have two bays at the southern end, one of which was regularly used by the boat trains from Dun Laoghaire. So, of course, it was the Dublin station best known by visitors from Britain and, in the days when Britain ruled Ireland, by civil servants, the military and politicians. The mail boats sailed from Dun Laoghaire, which was then called Kingstown, and the line was the very first railway in the land, opened in 1834. Westland Row had begun life as a terminus, the two main platforms only becoming through ones in 1891, when the City of Dublin Junction Railway was opened through to Amiens Street, one of the most, if not *the* most, important short sections of line in the country, as it linked all the routes to the southeast to the rest of the network.

Most of Westland Road's income came from its suburban business out along the highly desirable waterside districts of Sandymount, Blackrock, Seapoint, Sidney Parade, Booterstown, Salthill, Sandycove, Dalkey, Killiney and Bray. The latter also generated a huge amount of day-tripper business. It has to be said that CIÉ was woefully incompetent in making the most of this, and, between my first visit in 1959 and my second two years later, it actually closed Sidney Parade, Booterstown and Salthill. The arrival of the Dublin Area Rapid Transit (DART) electrified system in 1983 utterly changed everything. Indeed, without it, the city itself might have ground to a virtual standstill.

Apart from the suburban trains, long-distance ones also set off from Westland Row, southwards to Wicklow, Rosslare and Waterford, and westwards, by way of the Loop Line to Galway, Westport, Ballina, and Sligo. The first stop of the latter ones was at Amiens Street. Amiens Street was very much the liveliest and most interesting of Dublin's stations, with its three through platforms and three terminal ones.

The highly appropriately named DART system transformed commuting habits in the capital when it was inaugurated in 1984. It also saved the city streets from threatened gridlock. Two of the original Linke-Hofmann-Busch units are seen in 2010 skirting the Irish Sea between Dalkey and, in the distance, Killiney stations. This spectacular area of south Dublin, along the Vico Road with its beautiful villas, home of more than one world famous Irish pop star, above the railway line has been claimed to rival the Italian Riviera, with some justification, if one ignores the climate.

My next stop, by way of the GNR, was Belfast, where I travelled in 1961. I had earned even more as a holiday relief porter at Victoria than I had at Kings Cross, not least because there were wealthy clients off the Golden Arrow and the Night Mail from Paris. I once hit the jackpot by minding an entire holiday group's luggage, on a four-wheel barrow, for a whole hour for £10, which was equal to a week's wages. I could afford a seven-day all-Ireland rail ticket, which fitted with my great desire to return to Ireland and visit parts that I had not seen before. I arrived in Belfast, not from Dublin but from Omagh, courtesy of a former GNR AEC/Park Royal diesel railcar set, changing at Derry/Londonderry into a UTA unit made up of an astonishing variety of carriages, ranging from almost new open layout power cars to a trailer of purely 1920s Derby design, all with ornate beading and separate compartments.

I stepped out at York Road station, which still bore the scars of the fearful knocking about Belfast had received from Nazi bombs, and looked around me; I wondered for a moment if I had, by some magic carpet, been whisked across the Irish Sea, and deposited in Birkenhead, Bradford or, possibly, Manchester. Not only were there red pillar boxes and GPO vans, but also grand civic buildings, British banks, trolleybuses and, on the horizon, smoking chimneys and huge cranes. This was an industrial city writ large. The cranes and gantries belonged to the docks and to Harland and Woolf, builder of the Titanic and, at its busiest, employer of no fewer than 35,000 people, very few of them Roman Catholics, sometimes none. That statistic took an Englishman some getting his head around. How little I knew of what was part of my own country.

Belfast was home to three termini: York Road, which had been the property of the Northern Counties Committee (NCC) of the Midland, and later owned by London Midland and Scottish Railway; Great Victoria Street was GNR's home, although that too was now, strictly speaking, UTA property, as was the third; Queens Quay, which served Bangor on the coast, was the only surviving bit of the Belfast and County Down Railway. This company had been absorbed by the UTA in October 1948 and virtually its entire network, apart from the Bangor branch and a small stub, closed 15 months later. The last chairman, a realistic man, declared, 'an angel could not make the railway pay'.

The three termini were linked by the Harbour Commissioners line and Belfast Central Railway, the latter as important to Belfast as the Loop line was to Dublin. The LMS influence was apparent, both in a Fowler 0-6-0T shunting on the Harbour line at the back of York Road and the several Derby-built 2-6-4Ts I had spotted in and around the depot as we arrived from Derry. This depot would be the very last working steam one in the British Isles. Steam had long vanished from the vicinity of Queens Quay but was still evident when I managed to sneak into Adelaide depot, an impressive typical GNR yellow brick structure with black, brown and purple brick courses, and once home to 55 locomotives, making it one of the largest in the 32 Counties. There were fewer now but one was the VS 4-4-0 No 58 *Lagan*, which I had met two years earlier in Dublin. I would love to show you the photographs I took but I was using, perhaps, looking back, unadvisedly, a plate camera and managed to double expose all my Belfast pictures. I suppose if I had kept the negatives for some fifty years or more modern technology would have found a way of peeling the jumbled-up images apart but I did not and, as far as I know, it has not.

I left for Dublin next morning and was delighted to discover that my train was composed entirely of former GNR carriages, many of them wooden bodied, all in the sombre dark green UTA livery, and that, equally pleasing, our motive power, was steam; not a GNR 4-4-0, but one of the NCC 2-6-4Ts. I write, of course, as an enthusiast; your regular passenger might well have preferred a nice, shiny, light filled railcar. The NCC tanks were doing much of the remaining steam work on the GNR main line, across the border to Dundalk.

Dundalk, was, and is, a handsome station, as were so many GNR ones, but the works were the main attraction. I knew they had closed in the autumn of 1958, although many of the buildings remained and there was still work going on connected with buses and other road matters. A network of sidings remained and on it were parked a sad collection of GNR locomotives, awaiting breaking up. Most notable was *Merlin*, the last operational V Class Compound 4-4-0. Although it looked very much as if its working days were over and indeed it was sitting forlorn amongst a host of locomotives all of which were about to go under the breaker's torch, CIÉ still had a use for it, working the occasional passenger train between Dundalk and Dublin. The following year, Belfast Transport Museum declared that it hoped to acquire *Merlin* and, in March 1965, preparations were under way at Inchicore to get it ready for the journey to the North. A lengthy stay with Harland and Woolf resulted in its restoration and I, along with thousands of others, have been lucky enough to travel behind it on its old stamping ground between Dublin and Belfast and elsewhere.

A very different experience awaited back at the station where I found what looked like a typical American shunting locomotive in charge of my train for Dublin. It was a newly delivered, single cab grey painted Bo-Bo, and I had greatly misjudged it, for the 15 members of these 960hp General Motors (GM) locomotives were some of the best buys ever made. They were CIÉ's principal passenger locomotives in their early days, if not exactly overpowered for the task, and served faithfully for decades into the 21st century. Many more, of increasing power, would follow

I managed an invitation to Inchicore, CIÉ's principal works and depot which, of course, was utterly fascinating, if somewhat embarrassing as I was referred to throughout my visit as Professor Baker, a misapprehension I was unable to correct. It was the first of many visits over the years. The most thrilling was, perhaps, when accompanied by Maeve, we were invited by the late Charles Meredith, rail enthusiast, solicitor, jazz musician, and all-around good egg. He had played a leading role in the restoration of State Saloon, No 351, and had requested it be drawn out of its home within the works so that we could inspect it, inside and out, and pose for photographs.

Inevitably, as elsewhere in these islands, the manufacture of complete locomotives, carriages and wagons has long ceased at Inchicore; it looks rather tidier than when steam was king, and there is still much of interest going on.

Above: The interior of the State Saloon, with Maeve Baker and Charles Meredith sitting amongst the splendours of leather upholstery, magnificent panelling and lace curtains.

Left: Here is *Merlin*, at Dundalk, many years later, back in all its GNR glory, once again working the Enterprise from Belfast to Dublin.

Irish Railways

St. David, built by Cammell Laird for the Fishguard–Rosslare service on which it took up work in July 1947, is seen here proudly displaying its Great Western Railway coat of arms that it would wear for a brief six months before passing into the ownership of British Railways. At 3,352 tons, it was the successor of the 1932 vintage ship of the same name, also built in Birkenhead by Cammell Laird, which was lost by enemy action in Italy in January 1944.

There is no better way to start a holiday on the Emerald Isle than the voyage on the calm, blue, beautiful Irish Sea, communing with the seagulls and watching the passing ships. If it is very clear, when you are halfway across, you can spot both Wales and Ireland. We will gloss over the alternative scenario where nature decides to turn nasty – let us just say that I once spent more than 23 hours on a voyage across the Irish Sea during a gale force 12 one Christmas!

The boat train for Dublin is pulling out of Rosslare Europort in April 1989. The locomotive is an A Class Co-Co, built by Metropolitan Vickers in 1955–56; its Crossley power unit was replaced by a GM 1,250hp one in 1968–71. In the background are imported cars, and beyond them, a Sealink ferry from Fishguard and a Brittany ferry from Bilbao.

Wellington Bridge signal box on the line from Rosslare to Waterford in August 2007. The English Great Western Railway was part-owner of this line and promoted it as a rival to the LNWR's route to Ireland, by way of Holyhead and Kingstown (now Dún Laoghaire). Boat trains from there to Cork were a feature well into the 1980s. Traffic gradually fell away, and, in 2010, it ceased entirely, although the line is still maintained and there is a campaign to bring passenger traffic back. Wellington Bridge was a centre of the sugar beet business, a freight flow which ceased in 2006, but some of the wagons used were still there when this picture was taken.

A Limerick to Rosslare Harbour train crossing the Barrow Bridge, east of Waterford, 1 August 1986. The line opened in 1906 and the bridge, which was designed by Sir Benjamin Baker, is, at 2,131ft, the second longest in Ireland and the third longest rail bridge in the British Isles. The locomotive is No 186, a GM 1,150hp Bo-Bo of 1966, one of the workhorses upon which CIÉ relied for many decades.

No 157 sets off from Waterford to Wexford via Macmine Junction and New Ross in September 1959. A member of the celebrated J15 class, Ireland's most numerous steam locomotive type, this particular one lasted from 1889 until 1963 – not a bad investment, even if it did have a slightly bent frame in later life. Like the locomotive, its carriage is a splendid Edwardian clerestory roof composite of GS&WR origin. Just visible bringing up the rear is a typical example of Bulleid exotica, a four-wheel, unpainted guards van. Passenger traffic ended on this line in 1963, but freight continued between Waterford and New Ross until 1995.

Three small boys watch GM No 176, one the 1962-vintage 950hp Bo-Bos, shunting across the level crossing on the New Ross to Mullinavat Road at the Waterford end of New Ross on 24 August 1976.

The highly distinctive Waterford Central signal box, which is built across the tracks. Dating from the 1923 GS&WR days, it is in line for preservation, although it requires some renovation.

In May 2003, a 3ft gauge railway opened on the track bed of the former standard-gauge line from Waterford to Mallow. This was part of the route from Rosslare to Cork, and I recall travelling along it in a packed boat train in the summer of 1961. Unfortunately, business was not great outside of the holiday season, and the line closed in 1967, with the section to Ballinacourty, near Dungarvan, surviving for freight traffic until 1982. All was not lost, however, for a 10km line now runs along the Suir Valley, from Kilmeadan towards Waterford, and a train is seen here heading eastwards. More track was acquired from New Ross in 2020, and there is hope that eventually steam may reappear.

One of the more unusual locations in which to encounter a train was, and still is, along the quayside at Wexford. A train from Dublin is heading towards Rosslare, at little more than walking pace, past a preserved lightship, in 1969. The line opened in 1872 and is still there, although the quay has been rebuilt and extended so the track is now some distance from the water's edge.

Above left: Children lean over the footbridge at Enniscorthy in 2002. This is the next station to Wexford, heading north. Enniscorthy is an attractive town, the second largest in County Wexford, and features much in Irish history, most recently during the Easter Rising of 1916 when the railway line was cut, and rebels occupied the town. In the end, on instructions from James Connolly, the great trade unionist and commandant at the General Post Office in Dublin, both sides backed down and there was no bloodshed. Enniscorthy's cathedral, St Adan's, dates from 1843 and was the work of Pugin, designer of the London Houses of Parliament.

Above right: Wicklow in 2012 with No 186, one of the two preserved J15 former GS&WR 0-6-0s. Neither CIÉ nor its predecessor, GSR, had the money to spend on elaborate liveries and so they went to the other extreme and painted most of their locomotives in unlined grey, which quite often, and not surprisingly, was taken for a rather dull shade of black; although, it has to be said, No 186 does look rather fetching. No 186 is running around its train, which it has brought from Dublin.

Deep in a County Wicklow valley, former Dublin and South Eastern Railway (DSER) preserved 2-6-0 No 461, in charge of a rake of preserved CIÉ carriages in period green livery, takes on water at Rathdrum in 1992 with an enthusiasts' – there is a lot of them – special from Dublin to Rosslare. No 461 and its sister were built by Beyer Peacock in 1922, but because of the troubled times and a number of attacks on the railway system in this part of Ireland, they were sent north to Belfast for relative safety. Returning to their intended home area, they were often to be found working the heavy overnight Dublin freight trains, although they also did passenger work. No 461 outlived nearly all CIÉ's steam locomotives and, in 1967, was put on static display at Inchicore Works. Eventually, it was handed over to the Railway Preservation Society of Ireland (RPSI), which restored it to working order. No 461 is the only preserved inside-cylinder 2-6-0 in the British Isles.

Above: This is No 461 again, but this time, unlike preserved No 186, it looks very pretty in the green livery that CIÉ applied to certain locomotives in the immediate post-war years, completely transforming their appearance. Even if No 461 was not actually one of them, who cares? Certainly not its admirers at Kilkenny in August 2013!

Right: Kilkenny, August 2002. A Dublin-bound train has just arrived from Waterford. Whilst passengers find their seats, the locomotive, a GM 201 Class, will run around the train which will retrace its tracks as far as Lavistown, some two-and-a-half miles distant, where it will swing north-eastwards towards joining the Cork to Dublin main line at Cherryville Junction. Another 201 Class is at the far end of the station and there is a plentiful supply of Guinness in the goods yard. The Guinness no longer arrives by rail and passenger trains are now worked by railcars.

Left: Another, somewhat unlikely, survivor from a long time ago is this little tank engine, basking here in the sunshine in the 1980s. No 90 started out as the motive power of a railmotor built to operate the Castleisland branch in County Kerry and was converted into its present form in 1915. It worked first as a branch line engine and then as a shunter around Cork until withdrawal in 1961. Preservation came in 1967, initially at Fermoy and then, as seen here, at Mallow in 1983; the latter being the junction for the lines from Waterford and Tralee with the Dublin to Cork main line. More adventures would befall No 90 and we will meet it again later, restored to steam. My wife's grandmother recalled being told by her grandmother about her sighting of the royal train call at Mallow in August 1861, which stayed just long enough for Prince Albert to pull back the net curtain of their carriage so that Queen Victoria could wave at the assembled locals. The royal couple, like all good tourists, were on their way to Killarney and the Ring of Kerry.

Below: A Dublin to Cork express pulls out of Mallow station, 114.5km from Dublin, last stop before Cork, accelerating past Mallow South Cabin in August 2009. It is about to cross the lengthy Mallow Viaduct, which was destroyed during the Irish Civil War in 1922–23 and subsequently rebuilt. Immediately beyond it, the Killarney and Tralee line branches off to the west.

Although dieselisation was far advanced on CIÉ by the summer of 1959, it was still possible to come upon a shed scene such as this at Cork. Far left is 101 Class No 198, whilst there are no fewer than three of the MGWR K Class 0-6-0Ts dating from the 1890s, including No 552, which is in the centre track. The 0-6-0T was a relative rarity in Ireland, certainly compared with England, and the Ks were Ireland's most numerous, there being 12 in all. The big engine behind No 198 is one of the Woolwich Moguls, which was a Maunsell design, originally for the English SE&CR but were taken up by the government during World War One and built at Woolwich Arsenal. Far more were produced than were ever needed. MGWR, spotting a bargain, particularly one designed by Ireland's Maunsell, bought 26 of them. Being so cheap and coming from Woolwich, they inevitably acquired the nickname 'Woolworths'. Cheerfully expelling steam on the third track is a Beyer Peacock 4-6-0T built for the Cork, Bandon and South Coast Railway (CB&SCR), one of a class of eight excellent engines, which dated from 1906 to 1920 and were the last of that wheel arrangement in the British Isles.

Far and away the oldest locomotive on display at Cork in 1959, and still there today, was No 36 – Ireland's oldest surviving steam engine. Built in Liverpool by Bury, Curtis and Kennedy in 1847, it is a typical express engine of its time and lasted longer than most, being withdrawn in 1874. Its importance was recognised, although no one seemed to bother about its tender, and it has been exhibited around the country once or twice. No doubt the citizens of Cork are proud of it, but it might be even more fitting if such a unique survivor from so long ago be allocated an honoured home in the capital.

Irish Railways: The Last 60 Years

Above left: By the end of March 1961, the network of lines serving West Cork had disappeared, all except for the short stretch seen here, which served as a headshunt from the former CB&SCR Albert Quay station, reached via the Cork City Railway. A wide road now occupies the site.

Above right: This fine piece of art depicts one of the elegant CB&SCR 4-6-0Ts, which were the principal motive power in West Cork almost until the end of steam on the CB&SCR system.

One of the most impressive structures to be found on the edge of Roaring Water Bay in West Cork is this viaduct at Ballydehob, built by the narrow-gauge Schull & Skibbereen Tramway and operated between 1886 and 1947.

Ten express passenger four-cylinder 4-6-0s were designed by E A Watson and put into service between 1914 and 1922. They proved far from satisfactory, and, consequently, all were substantially rebuilt and three were scrapped. This was a financial disaster for the company, which was struggling under the debt imposed by Britain after Eire gained its independence in 1921. This is No 402, the most rebuilt, and probably the best of the rebuilds, preparing to tackle the fearsome gradient out of Cork with the overnight goods train for Dublin in September 1959. No 402 was the last survivor of this type, being withdrawn in 1961.

No 801 *Macha* has just left the 1,355-yard-long tunnel outside Glanmire Road station, Cork, and is heading up the 1 in 60 climb with a lightweight goods train bound for Thurles on 2 September 1961. *Macha* was one of three huge Class B1a three-cylinder 4-6-0 locomotives designed by E C Bredin specifically for the Dublin to Cork route. They were, unlike their predecessors, immediately successful, proving powerful and fast. Unfortunately, World War Two and the shortages imposed upon Ireland brought their gallop to an untimely end. The first of this type, No 800 *Maedb*, instantly became, and remains, Ireland's most famous locomotive, and is preserved in Cultra in Belfast. However, before the three sisters could really prove themselves in the post-war world, dieselisation ensued, and they were reduced to such mundane tasks as seen here. No 802 was withdrawn in 1957, and its two sisters in 1962.

Top: Cobh Junction. The most direct route between Cork City and the transatlantic port of Cobh (formerly Queenstown) is by rail rather than road, and here A58R has charge of a Cobh-bound train as it swings through the junction with the Youghal branch in 1970. This later closed in 1988 but was reopened as far as Midleton in 2009.

Above: Cobh station in August 1996. It was from Queenstown/Cobh that millions of Irish men, women and children sailed away for a new life on the other side of the Atlantic, boarding a tender alongside the station out to the liner waiting for them in mid channel. This Tokyu-built railcar, No 2611, dating from 1994, was from the first of the new generation of Irish Rail railcars from Japan.

Left: A statue in Cobh of Annie Moore and her two brothers. Annie Moore was the first person through Ellis Island's gates when the facility opened in New York in 1892.

Above left: An only slightly posed picture of an Irish colleen (girl). Tourists arriving by the GWR Fishguard to Rosslare route might, in Edwardian times, expect to find them thronging the streets of Killarney in their dozens, possibly assisted by the tourist board.

Above right: After all that excitement, there was only one venue to which tourists could retire for sustenance, rest, and comfort and that, of course, was Killarney's finest hotel, courtesy of Great Southern Railway.

Tourists would also find that motor transport had not penetrated that part of County Kerry.

Quite possibly the highlight for the local children of Castleisland, Co Kerry, during the seemingly endless summer holidays in the early 1970s was the arrival and the subsequent shunting of the daily freight train from Tralee. Castleisland was at the end of a four-and-a-half-mile branch from Gortatlea on the line from Mallow and Killarney to Tralee. The branch opened in 1875 and was initially worked by a railmotor, the motive part we have already met sitting on the platform at Mallow. The branch closed on 10 January 1977, though the local travel agents still advertised a connection to Cobh where a Transatlantic Cunard liner could be boarded.

Old and New. In 1972, CIÉ introduced a fleet of air-conditioned British Rail Mark 2D carriages, built at Derby Works. A considerable leap forward in design for CIÉ, they were named Supertrains. A rake is standing here in the sidings at Tralee in August 1973, whilst opposite is a goods train consisting mostly of cattle wagons. Moving cattle around the country by rail was still big business, but it would come to an end in 1974.

Oops! As always, whenever something goes wrong, an informal committee immediately assembles to apportion blame, suggest solutions and generally get under everyone's feet. Such would seem to be the situation here on a wet day in Tralee in the early 1970s. The relatively minor angle of the derailed cattle wagon would suggest that no animals were harmed in the process.

Right: Back in the 1970s, there were still quite extensive sidings at Tralee. Pictured here are two small boys observing an 001 Class locomotive going about its business at Rock Street yard. The Tralee passenger station is out of sight in the distance to the left, whilst the North Kerry line to Listowel and Limerick, and the branch to Fenit, continue past the photographer. The terminus of the narrow-gauge Tralee and Dingle Railway was to the right of the tall building where there were interchange sidings.

Below: The 3ft gauge Tralee and Dingle Railway operated through what I, as a perhaps biased author, considers the finest scenery in Ireland. It opened in 1892 and was a boon to the community of the Dingle Peninsular, but, with the influx of the motor vehicle in the 1920s, it could not really compete, and passenger traffic ceased in 1939. The cattle business survived until 1953. Hunslet 2-6-2T No 5T took itself off to the Cavan and Leitrim Railway and, eventually, like so many inhabitants of this part of Kerry, to the US. However, somewhat miraculously, it came home many decades later. Three kilometres of track was laid from the outskirts of Tralee to Blenerville, where the Dingle Peninsular begins, and here, No 5T, probably feeling in the soft, gentle rain like it had never left home, is doing what it was trained for. Sadly, it has not run since 2006 and needs remedial boiler work.

Fenit in 1980. The mountains of the Dingle Peninsular, at the foot of which the Castlegregory branch of the Tralee and Dingle Railway ran until 1939, loom in the distance over Tralee Bay. The Tralee to Fenit branch opened in 1887 and was closed to regular passenger traffic in 1934. However, it had a long twilight existence of another 42 years with the occasional passenger excursion, as well as regular freight, some of which served the once busy harbour. A CIÉ Leyland Leopard bus awaits to return to Tralee. Today, there is scarcely any form of public transport to or from Fenit, other than for school children and one bus in each direction on Fridays.

Ardfert station in August 1975. Anyone in search of the most typical deeply rural, remote, wayside station in all of Ireland would have found Ardfert exactly what they were looking for. That is until January 1977, when the daily goods train officially called for the very last time, although one suspects that that the actual last time any business had disturbed the flora and fauna, which had come to regard Ardfert's single platform as their exclusive territory, was some weeks earlier. Ardfert station opened in 1880. It was situated on the North Kerry line, linking Tralee with Limerick, six-and-a-half miles from Tralee, just beyond where the Tralee and Fenit lines diverged, and 17½ miles from Listowel; it was also within a brisk walk of some wonderful beaches. It closed to passengers in July 1963. The quite substantial station building – indeed, far more substantial when it was built than many of the surrounding cottages – survives as a four-bedroom holiday let.

General Motors Bo-Bo No B150 climbs away from Tralee towards Ardfert with the daily North Kerry freight, calling at all stations to Listowel and Limerick, in August 1973.

The up and down North Kerry goods trains meet at Listowel in August 1971, each hauled by a re-engined A Class. The North Kerry line, connecting Tralee with Limerick, was opened fully in 1880. Listowel, although of no great size – the population at last count was 4,820 – is the cultural (it has produced some terrific, world-renowned writers), administrative, business and agricultural centre for a large part of Kerry, and for the best part of 80 years, the railway served it well and was vital to its prosperity. My wife's uncle, Paddy Finucane, was the independent TD (MP) there for many years. By the time of my first visit in 1969, regular passenger traffic had ended six years previously, but, as you can see, there was plenty of freight business.

Above left: Another uncle, Willy, who ran the family farm, used to do a competition in the Sunday paper that involved putting in correct order ten young fashionably dressed ladies. One Monday morning, to everyone's utter surprise, including his own, he discovered he was the winner and the prize, a brand-new Austin Mini, arrived at his door, replacing the donkey that he took to the creamery in Listowel each morning. How could the railway compete with that?

Above right: The Lartigue was a monorail, the invention of a Frenchman of that name who brought it to Kerry in 1888, much to the astonishment of all who saw and travelled upon it. It connected Listowel with the seaside resort of Ballybunion, nine miles distant and famous for its wonderful, but potentially treacherous, Atlantic rollers. The basic principle was that the train ran along a single, central rail and was supported either side by two others. It lasted for some 36 years, but GSR, on its formation in 1925, took one look and shut it down. During subsequent years, it attracted an almost legendary status and cousin, Micky Barry, who owned a farm over which the Lartigue had run, devoted himself to its memory. He, along with farmer friends, assiduously preserved every buried metal artefact they ploughed up, and, eventually, in the early 1970s, was able to present this wonderful reconstruction.

Such was the Lartigue's enduring fame that a campaign to bring it back gathered much support, including that of the local TD, a retired famous Gaelic footballer. Here we see the press photographing Grandad Finucane who, at the age of 100, was invited to take a ride, something he had first done some 90 years earlier. When asked for his impression of the original, he remarked that it was, 'a dreadful old thing, which rattled and bumped and could be easily overtaken by lads like ourselves on our bikes'. For these remarks, he was severely scolded by his wife who said: 'That's not the sort of thing you should be saying to the press.' The new Lartigue is 1km long, and at Listowel, on the site of the original, there is a diesel-powered 0-3-0 replica of the original steam train, built in 2003 by Alan Keef.

Original Lartigue. A delightful picture that must have been taken very late on, probably just before closure in 1925; note the broken window. Clearly posed for the camera, one wonders if these were visiting tourists. Either way, it nicely illustrates how one crossed from one side to the other and that, from the side, the style of the carriages looked very much of their period.

Foynes, the hometown of my mother-in-law, was still busy with freight in 1971, although the passenger service from Limerick had ended in February 1963. A port near the mouth of the Shannon, the branch from Limerick opened in April 1858. Although freight ceased running to the port in October 2000, the track is still in place and there is much scope for freight to be revived for the group of ports near the mouth of the Shannon and inland to Limerick, which together form the second busiest group of ports in the Republic.

For a brief period, from the late 1930s until 1946, Foynes became one of the world's most important traffic hubs. A flying boat service between it and Newfoundland began in 1937 and, with the outbreak of war, it became of vast strategic value, enabling the likes of Winston Churchill to fly direct across the Atlantic, the flight taking between 12 and 15½ hours. Later, flying boats were able to extend their range as far as New York, although the journey could take 25 hours. With the end of the war, and the construction of Shannon Airport on the opposite bank of the river in 1946, which served land-based airliners, the flying boat era came to an end. A full-size replica of one of the flying boats forms part of the fascinating museum, including the original control tower, which brings many visitors to Foynes.

The 4-4-0 locomotive had played a significant part in the story of the passenger train in Ireland, and although only five had been built since 1925 by GSR, CIÉ in its early years still employed them on top link passenger duties, and on just about every branch line. However, dieselisation swiftly wiped them out and the last departed in 1960. In this scene at Limerick on 7 September 1959, two are awaiting breaking up. D14 No 93 of 1885–95 stands ahead of D4 No 342 of 1936. Three GNR and one NCC 4-4-0s have been preserved but none from any of the railways that became part of GSR has been.

There was clearly much freight activity going on in the Limerick area in this early 1970s view, which looks eastwards away from the station, the standard CIÉ brake van being prominent. A re-engined A Class can be seen in the distance, while a GM Bo-Bo is on the right. A CIÉ Atlantean double-decker bus is crossing the bridge spanning the tracks.

Radio Train was a popular initiative of CIÉ between the 1950s and 1970s, operating three days a week in the summer months from Dublin either to Galway (Connemara) or Killarney, with the radio providing music, entertainment and a commentary on the scenery broadcast to every passenger. Here, in the charge of A40R, *Radio Train* speeds past Limerick Junction in August 1970 on its way to Killarney.

In 1971, a Dublin to Cork express performs the famous manoeuvre at Limerick Junction that surely inspired Riverdance, as it shimmies out of the station's one through platform to continue on its way. Two GMs provide the motive power, and the leading carriages are newly delivered Cravens. Waiting to take its place is a non-rebuilt A Class loco, which is busying itself shunting a Bullied-era open wagon about the establishment.

Passengers relax as they await their connection at Limerick Junction in August 1975.

Passengers are in a hurry at Limerick Junction in 2011. On the right is a train from Limerick city, and a Dublin-bound express is on the left.

Kilkee in August 1975. The Atlantic outpost of the 3ft narrow-gauge West Clare Railway, the station and the entire network closed in February 1961. However, as you can see, the station was still pretty well intact, with a family disporting themselves on the platform when this picture was taken 14 years after closure.

One of the West Clare locomotives, No 5 *Slieve Callan* of 1892, was preserved and was mounted in the yard of Ennis station, where the West Clare connected with the standard-gauge line from Limerick to Galway. There it spent decades before being rescued, restored to steam and set to work on a short section of the re-laid West Clare system at Moyasta Junction, where it was photographed in 2013.

The Galway to Clifden branch had a very short existence. It opened in the summer of 1895, and the hope was that the tourists would come flocking to enjoy the glorious Connemara scenery. To this end, through carriages from Dublin to Clifden were attached to Galway trains. However, the hoped-for bonanza never arrived, and the line shut in April 1935, before the season even had a chance to get going one last time. Such was the remoteness and lack of development in Connemara, that when this picture was taken in August 1969 of Maeve – who had spent eight years being educated by the nuns at Kylemore Abbey in a very remote part of Connemara – communing with the donkeys, it was very easy to trace the trackbed, as seen here on the opposite side of the lake and beyond the donkeys, all the way to Clifden.

Clifden in 1969. An almost complete set of buildings and facilities still survived here more than 30 years after the last train had pulled out. I would have liked to record Alcock and Brown, who landed nearby after the world's first flight across the Atlantic in 1919, as they travelled from here back to Dublin by train, but, apparently, they were met by motor car. Shades of things to come.

Galway on 7 September 1959. Former MGWR G2 2-4-0 No 653 shunts in the goods yard. This was probably the most useful class of 2-4-0s ever built. Dating from 1893, the class was described by Clements and Robbins in their *ABC of Irish Locomotives*, published in 1949, as 'probably the last class of 2-4-0 in existence in which no engine has yet been scrapped', except for a Civil War victim. Equally at home on passenger and goods work, it outlived all the GSR 4-4-0s inherited by CIÉ, with No 653 proving to be the very last, being withdrawn in 1962. Oh, that it had been preserved!

Pictured from the platform end at Galway station on a summer evening in the 1990s. By this time, the tracks curving to the left beyond the platform had become sidings, but the one on the far left was all that was left of the Clifden branch; trains heading through Connemara had to reverse out of the station. Beyond, the main line curves to the left to cross Lough Atalia, and beyond that lies Galway Bay.

G613 is at the head of the branch line train from Loughrea, which will connect with a Dublin to Galway train. The nine-mile-long branch from Loughrea to Attymon Junction was opened in December 1890 and was worked from the beginning by MGWR. Our family was staying at Kilkee for the month of August 1975, and I took the opportunity, with my three-year-old son, William, to drive to Loughrea and ride the branch and then on to Galway. Officially, the train was described as mixed, and, on this occasion, the one piece of freight was a parcel, which the guard deposited at Dunsandle, the only intermediate station. The line was also described as 'Ireland's last genuine branch'. It seemed quite busy, and I assumed its future was assured, so I was somewhat taken aback to discover the following month that it was to close, which it did on 3 November of that year, thus reducing yet further the opportunities for the little Deutz G Class four wheelers to find gainful employment. There were ten of them, the first three delivered in 1956–57 with 140hp, followed by a further seven in 1962 with 160hp and were, quite honestly, a waste of money – the branch lines they might have worked were wiped out before many of them had even set wheels on Irish soil!

The harvesting of turf on an industrial scale became a huge undertaking after the setting up of Bora na Móna (The Irish Turf Board) in 1933, most of it in the Midland counties east of Athlone. Near Portlaoise, turf is being loaded onto one of the 3ft gauge lines, without which the industry could not function. Note the power station in the distance. Environmental issues have brought about great changes, but the smell of turf burning in a country cottage fire is an abiding memory.

Above: It is fascinating how a change of livery can transform a locomotive. The 18 2,250hp GM 071 Class Co-Cos arrived in 1976 and took over all the principal long distance passenger duties. Gradually, they moved to freight and infrastructure duties, and, in 2006, a number were repainted in this attractive, short-lived livery. No 075 is seen here in 2010 at Portarlington, in charge of a train of ballast hoppers – I think it is clear who owns these!

Left: A busy scene at Claremorris. Claremorris is used to such scenes, for it was once the junction of no fewer than five routes: to the west the Ballinrobe branch; to the northwest the main line to Westport and Ballina; to the northeast to Collooney and Sligo; to the southeast the main line to Athlone and Dublin; and due south to Tuam and Athenry. At one time, the route, known as the 'Western Corridor', extended from Limerick, through Ennis, Athenry and Claremorris to Sligo, but all passenger traffic had ceased by 1976. However, the section between Limerick and Ennis reopened tentatively in 1988, but it gradually prospered until there were nine trains in each direction daily, followed by the reinstatement of the section to Athenry in 2010. Plans for any further openings have stalled.

Above left: For a time in the 1990s, a preservation group took up residence at Tuam and, apart from a number of 1950s-era CIÉ carriages, restored to their original green livery, and one 121 Class GM, seen here, they also briefly operated the preserved former Castleisland 0-6-0T No 90, now at Downpatrick, on the main line.

Above right: A Westport to Dublin train composed of BR-built Mark 2Ds and hauled by a 201 Class GM is about to depart a rather damp Claremorris in 2005. The track to the right is the disused section of the Western Corridor to Athenry. There was a time when vast numbers of pilgrims to the nearby Knock Shrine would arrive at Claremorris by train and CIÉ operated a number of specially adapted carriages for the disabled.

A Westport to Dublin train hauled by a 071 Class locomotive prepares to call at Manulla Junction. This is one of a small number of stations in the British Isles that have no road access and are there purely to effect a change of trains, in this case the 20-mile branch to Ballina. Trains began running between Dublin and Westport in 1866 and from Manulla Junction to Ballina in 1873.

Two GMs sit prettily amongst the light and shade of Sligo's somewhat neglected and rather too-big-for-purpose station, having arrived from Dublin in August 1993. The leading one is a member of the original single cab 121 Class, delivered in 1961, the other is a later double cab 141 Class. Sligo was once also the terminus of trains from Limerick and Galway, and also for those of Sligo, Leitrim & Northern Counties Railway (SL&NCR), the latter of which was much occupied with the cattle business, which it handed over to GNR at Enniskillen. The closure of the GNR line through Enniskillen in 1957 sounded the death knell of SL&NCR, although, remarkably, one of its steam locomotives has been preserved, as has a diesel railcar, although that one requires a huge effort to restore its rather sad remains.

Donegal Town station dates from 1889 and is now a museum devoted to the narrow-gauge railway, which served Ireland's most northwest county from 1863 to 1960. The County Donegal Railway was, in its way, a wonderful railway and managed to fight off road transport competition for years before finally succumbing, with CIÉ buses eventually taking over.

County Donegal Railway, owned jointly by the NCC and the GNR, was an enthusiastic pioneer of the diesel railcar and it is fortunate that several have survived and even more fortunate that this one, No 18, dating from 1940, offers a three-mile ride at Fintown through wonderful Donegal scenery.

Since 1961, residents and visitors desiring public transport in County Donegal have had to make do with buses, and not a lot of those as time has passed. Here, a Bus Éireann coach heads away from Glencomcille for Donegal town in 2010.

The other narrow-gauge railway of significance serving Donegal was the Londonderry and Lough Swilly Railway. It embraced road transport a good deal earlier than County Donegal Railway and, as a consequence, lasted much longer. Mail buses were a feature in Donegal, and here a Lough Swilly Leyland Tiger Cub has arrived at the Downings in 1976. It finally ceased operations, still calling itself the Londonderry and Lough Swilly Railway Company, in April 2014.

Dromod is yet another venue where proof exists that after 1960 the narrow gauge was not dead, but merely sleeping. On the right is the Irish Rail station, on the Dublin to Sligo line, whilst on the left is where trains connected with the Cavan and Leitrim Railway, which closed originally on 31 March 1959. The preservationists moved in at the end of 1992 and much has happened since then; track has been re-laid, with steam putting in an appearance, and there is, as seen here, a genuine former Tralee and Dingle carriage, No 10T, built in Bristol in 1891. To the right are the frames of another Tralee and Dingle carriage.

On a day when the early morning frost refused to disappear, the day mail from Dublin to Galway, hauled by Metrovick Co-Co No 020 pauses at Mullingar on 31 December 1979. In those days, the route taken was by the former MGWR main line from Pearse station by way of the loop line, past Liffey Junction and on from Mullingar to Athlone.

Mullingar was where old railway trains went to die. In this 1995 view are a number of Bulleid's triangulated wagon frames, several CIÉ standard goods brake vans, and a great variety of other wagons, plus at least two carriages, one in black and orange, the other in departmental grey. The still intact but little-used track of the old MGWR main line to Galway is seen passing between the rows of scrap vehicles.

Originally, Navan was served both by GNR and MGWR. Passenger traffic is long gone, but there is an excellent case for reviving a commuter service to Dublin and easing road traffic congestion. 071 Class-hauled freight is a regular feature in the shape of zinc ore trains from Tara mines to Dublin Port, as seen here at a level crossing in the town in 2014.

Above: The Downpatrick and County Down Railway is a wonderful example of what preservationists can achieve, although the COVID-19 lockdowns have done it no favours. We have met this little former GS&WR 0-6-0T, No 90, before, and it is seen here up north, hauling handsome GS&WR bogie carriage No 1097, passing a reconstructed signal box. This is a typical NCC structure, with distinctive overhanging eaves, that had stood at King's Bog on the Bleach Green to Antrim line, and was moved from there in 1991.

Right: The interior of carriage No 1097. Since restoration by the RPSI, this 1925-vintage GSR (but of pure GS&WR design) corridor tri-composite has spent time working out of Whitehead on the main line and also at Downpatrick. It is typical of many thousands of such carriages of that era, which could be found on main line passenger trains throughout the length and breadth of the British Isles. Such carriages were still at work in Ireland into the 1970s.

Former GNR S Class 4-4-0 No 171 *Slieve Gullion*, designed and built by Beyer Peacock in 1913, at Belfast Central in 1993.

Ulster Transport Museum, Cultra, Belfast. Ireland's most powerful locomotive, GSR 4-6-0 No 800 *Maedb* of 1939, and NCC of the LMS 4-4-0 No 1924 *Dunluce Castle*.

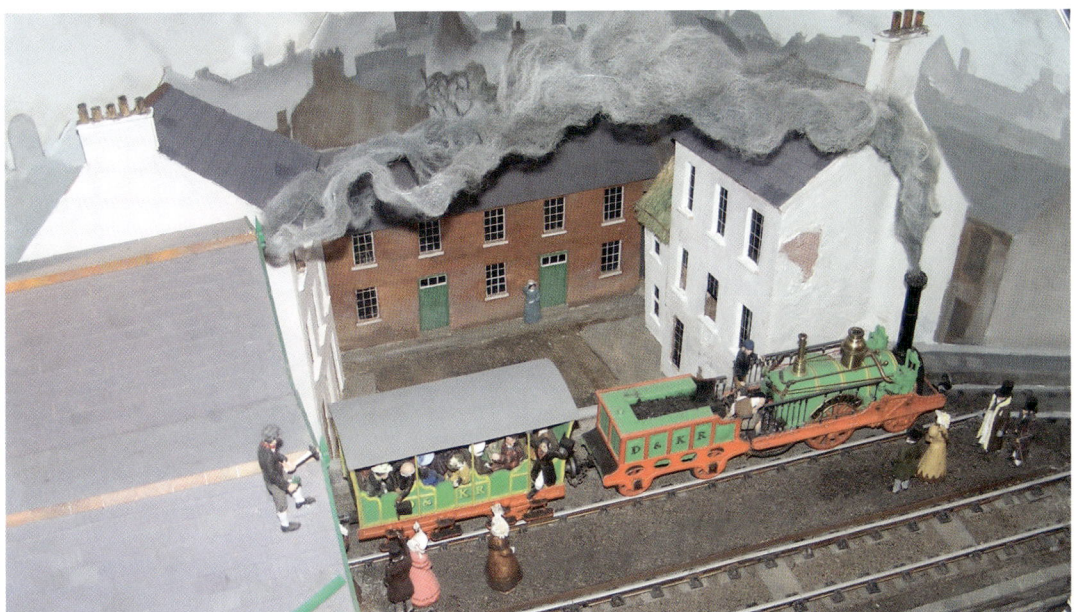

Cultra has this charming model of Ireland's very first railway, the Dublin and Kingstown of 1834. No expense was spared when the transport part of the Ulster Folk and Transport Museum opened in 1993, showcasing a vast and imaginatively displayed collection of locomotives, carriages, wagons, trams, trolleybuses, and so much else from all of Ireland.

Witham Street, Belfast, was the home of the original collection. It was cramped, and it was difficult to get a clear view of the exhibits. But, and it is a huge but, we should all be eternally grateful to those early pioneers who, with little official encouragement, saved much, not least from the narrow-gauge lines, which were on the verge of extinction. One such was No 2 *Kathleen*, a 4-4-0T of 1887 from the Cavan and Leitrim Railway and one of that line's carriages. As you can see, the carriage then was unrestored, although it is now pristine in Cultra.

Left: Amongst the many road exhibits in Cultra are this tram and trolleybus from Belfast. The tram is No 357 of 1930, whilst in the distance is the big, six-wheeler trolleybus, No 112, which ran from 1948 to 1968. Belfast possessed the only trolleybus system in Ireland. It was actually the second biggest in the British Isles, after London.

Below: By the summer of 1969, main line steam was a thing of the past in England, Wales and Scotland. However, in Northern Ireland, it was still possible to encounter regular steam passenger workings. On a bright, early September evening, Derby-built WT Class 2-6-2T No 4 is about to set off for Belfast from Larne Harbour, having earlier brought in a commuter train from the city. The WTs, of 1946–47, although clearly related to the long line of LMS 2-6-4Ts, were also derived from the pre-war NCC W Class 2-6-0s. The leading carriage is a former North Atlantic Express corridor brake vehicle of 1934. Both locomotive and carriage have been preserved.

A few minutes later, No 4 makes its presence felt as it rounds the long inlet from the Irish Sea on its way towards Belfast.

A multi-liveried 80 Class three-car unit departs from Larne Harbour and is Belfast bound in August 1984. These diesel-electric units, dating from 1974 to 1978, were built at Derby and were based on BR Mark 2C vehicles. The ferry for Stranraer can be seen on the left in the distance.

A night view of Larne Harbour station and a Spanish-built 4000 Class railcar set of 2011–12 about to leave in December 2014, seen from the deck of the Cairn Ryan (successor to Stranraer) ferry.

Above: Whitehead was really the creation of the railway of the late Victorian and Edwardian eras and developed into a delightful small resort on Belfast Lough, looking across towards Bangor. The station and the beautifully kept houses facing the sea are, not surprisingly, a conservation area.

Left: Trains run every hour from Belfast to Whitehead, the journey taking 35 minutes. A 3000 Class three-car unit railcar is arriving in September 2014. There currently are 23 of these units, all built by CAF at Zaragoza, Spain, in 2004–05.

It is not an understatement to claim that Whitehead has become world renowned as the home of the Railway Preservation Society of Ireland. Founded in 1964, it is fitting that its headquarters, visitor centre, and workshop should be at Whitehead, based on what were the sidings for excursion trains. Its achievements, throughout what have sometimes been the most difficult circumstances, across all 32 Counties, have been extraordinary. Here, the restoration of No 131 *Uranus*, a GNR Glasgow-built Q Class of 1901 is nearing completion, a task brought to fruition in 2017 when it became the third GNR 4-4-0 to return to main line work.

The RPSI not only restores main locomotives but carriages too, of course, and here 1932-vintage Compound No 85 *Merlin* has charge of LMS NCC No 91, a corridor brake first of 1934, built for the prestigious businessman's North Atlantic Express and Great Southern Railways corridor of 1921.

Right: Each December, Whitehead holds a street festival in which the RPSI takes part, and here in 2014, they are demonstrating that the RPSI embraces not only steam but diesel as well.

Below: In 1883, an electric powered narrow-gauge tramway, the first electric railway in Ireland, opened, running seven miles from the resort of Portrush to Giant's Causeway. It closed in 1949, but a much-shortened successor, seen here, started operating in 2002 using, initially, equipment from Lord O'Neill's railway at Shane's Castle.

Left: Steam can also sometimes be seen; this dear little Bristol-built Peckett 0-4-0 tank engine, *Tyrone*, dates from 1904 and spent most of its life working for British Aluminium at Larne. Withdrawn in 1960, it then went to Lord O'Neill's railway and from there to Giant's Causeway.

Below: Tourists from all over the world disport themselves amongst some of the 40,000 basalt columns that form Giant's Causeway, Northern Ireland's only UNESCO-recognised World Heritage Site.

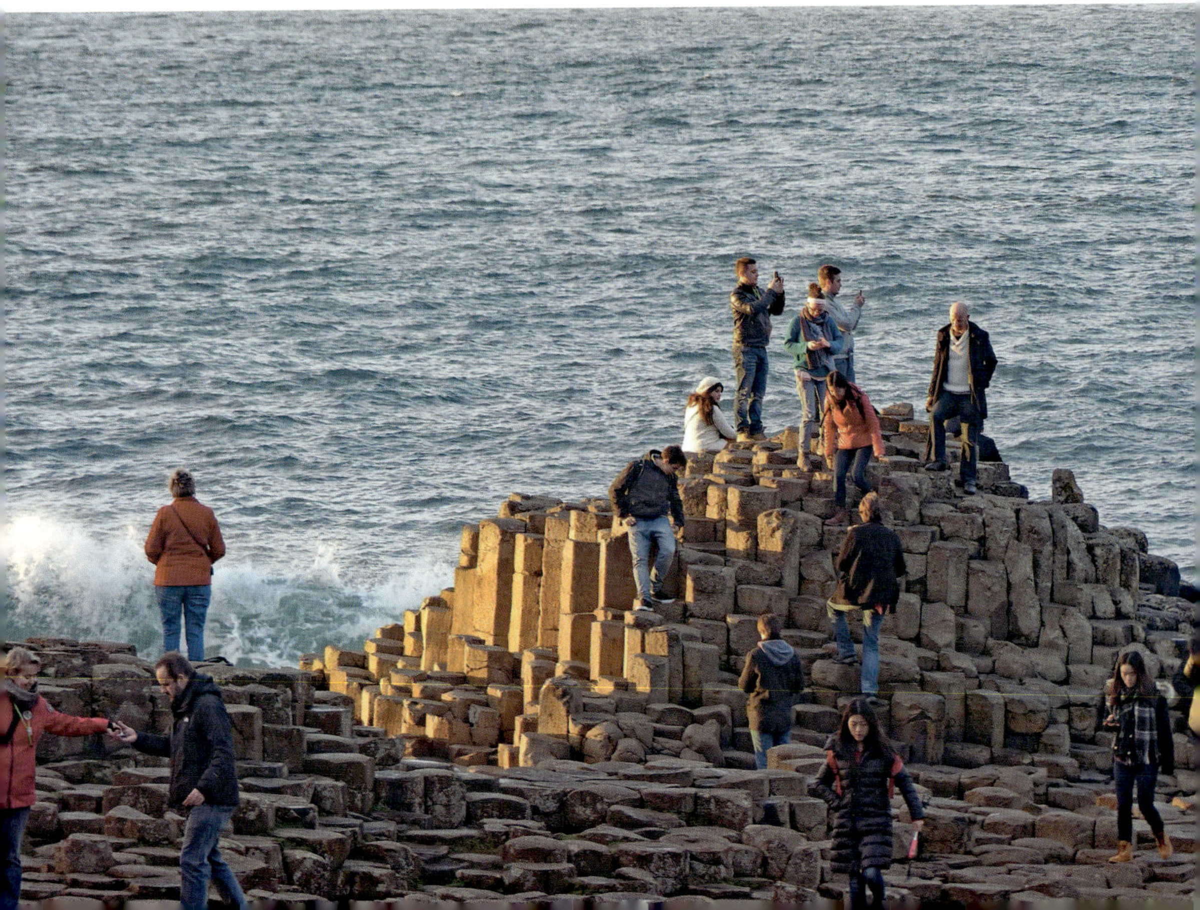

Right: Portrush grew, with the assistance of both the railway and Giant's Causeway, in Victorian times into Northern Ireland's most popular resort. The original station of 1855 was replaced by this very much grander one in 1893. The Giant's Causeway line terminated in the street alongside it. During the hard times of the last decades of the 20th century, the station was much neglected and might well have been demolished. Fortunately, other uses were found for it and, in 2019, a more modest, but striking, new station was opened behind it to cater for travellers arriving for golf's Open Championship.

Below: Edwardian visitors pose, in an appropriately dignified manner, at Portrush in 1910 as the steamer TSS *Hazel* sets out for Ardrossan. Portrush was a particular favourite with Scottish visitors.

Portrush was not only popular with holidaymakers but also with well-off Belfast businessmen and their families, and, in the 1930s, a train for businessmen, the North Atlantic Express, was equipped with especially designed carriages and took just 74 minutes non-stop, leaving Portrush at 08.10 and arriving at York Road, Belfast, at 09.30. In the 1970s, the RPSI revived the idea, and since then, during most summers, it has recreated the non-stop journey with the *Portrush Flyer*. It is photographed here, hauled by WT 2-6-4T No 4, seen leaving Portrush in August 1979.

Left: Ballymoney was once the junction for the narrow-gauge line to Ballycastle. This closed in 1950, and buses now park beside its platform. Rebuilt at the beginning of the 20th century, Ballymoney was then refurbished at the beginning of the 21st century, and this is the attractive main platform. Note the pillarbox.

Below: Coleraine is the junction for the Portrush branch and is therefore rather important, for there are few enough junctions left in the 6 Counties.

The station dates from 1855 but has been much modernised and greatly improved, the old blending skilfully with the new. A row of handsome original cast iron pieces supports the awning on the down platform.

The exterior of the down side of the station, carefully restored. Note the emphasis on Translink, the Northern Ireland Transport Company that oversees all road and rail public transport provision in the 6 Counties, encouraging interchange between road and rail, and even now still handles parcels.

A Derry/Londonderry to Belfast train passing Downhill, along the most picturesque section of the entire route. There was a little-used station here between 1853 and 1976. The tower dominating the view was the library of the Earl of Bristol, built in the late 18th century and now owned by the National Trust, whilst in the far distance across the water some lucky person in Portrush may be finding a crock of gold at the end of the rainbow.

Derry/Londonderry once was generously provided with no less than four stations. One was that of the County Donegal Railway, which closed on 31 December 1954, but reminders of it were provided for a time afterwards by the North West of Ireland Railway Society, with this short Donegal train parked on a section of track beside the still extant station building on the east bank of the River Foyle. It consists of one of the celebrated Red Vans, which were used to carry goods in locked vans across the border to avoid customs duties between Northern Ireland and the Republic, a third-class carriage and a 2-6-4T.

The GNR station was on the west bank of the Foyle. On my one and only journey there in September 1961, I arrived from Omagh in a GNR railcar that had set out from Belfast, and, getting out my sketchbook, I crossed the bridge over the Foyle and drew the scene and watched two steam-hauled freight trains arrive. On 15 February 1965, the GNR line closed, leaving the former NCC line the only one still serving Northern Ireland's second city. Later, in 1990, the Foyle Valley Railway Museum opened on the site of the tracks leading to the GNR station. New, 3ft narrow-gauge tracks were laid alongside the Foyle with the intention that they would reach as far as the border with the Republic, thus creating the almost unique phenomenon of a preserved line operating in two countries. When this picture was taken of the preserved County Donegal railcar No 12 setting off from the museum, all seemed to be well, but the line was never extended and, sadly, the museum closed in 2002. It later reopened in 2017.

My drawing of the city and the Foyle Bridge.

Above left: The sad looking and damp closed museum at Derry/Londonderry, with a preserved Donegal 2-6-4T outside, in 2010. The engine has since received a cosmetic restoration and the museum reopened on an occasional basis.

Above right: Ticket checking at Derry in 2014.

This is the yard of Londonderry and Lough Swilly Railway at Letterkenny in 1977, where all sorts of relics could be found, including this carriage gradually being absorbed by the undergrowth, an AEC lorry and a Leyland Royal Tiger bus.

Strabane was where GNR and County Donegal Railway met, but by the time I took this picture in 1977, all that was left of the railway scene was the rusting remains of a County Donegal 2-6-4T and a number of carriage underframes. When County Donegal Railway closed down, an American, Dr Cox, arranged to buy much of the rolling stock and track and ship it all across the Atlantic. However, this never happened, although a few items were eventually rescued and remain in Ireland. Travellers were living on the site, which was pretty much in no man's land between Northern Ireland and the Republic. You can see some of their washing in and around the locomotive and, in the background, at least one caravan.

No 33, one of the big GNR SG3 0-6-0s of 1920–21, shunting at Omagh in September 1959. Renumbered from GNR 20, it lasted until 1965. Omagh was where the Portadown to Derry/Londonderry train met the line from Bundoran and Enniskillen.

Reminders that Greenore, like Rosslare far away to the south, owed its existence as a port partly to investment by an English railway company, this time LNWR. The cattle traffic was its chief business.

Above left: Two lines ran out of Greenore to Dundalk and Newry and were worked by six-saddle tanks based on Ramsbottom's DX 0-6-0 goods engines. The LNWR also sent over wagons and carriages, and these lasted post-1945. However, the cattle trade had fallen drastically, from 114,000 head in 1938 to a mere 6,800 in 1949, and both lines, now owned by the British Transport Commission, closed on 31 December 1951. This is a scene at the former station at Carlingford in 2009, during an international festival organised across the border at Newry.

Above right: One of the Ramsbottom saddle tanks and several of the carriages remained at work until the end, but the passenger traffic was mostly in the hands of GNR 2-4-2Ts. One carriage and GNR J2 No 93 have been preserved and are seen here at Cultra.

Belfast is set amongst fine scenery. This is the view looking north from a train passing Holywood on its way from Belfast to Bangor.

Seen from the north bank of Belfast Lough, a Stena Line ferry from Cairn Ryan is rounding Carrickfergus in 2014 and heading for Belfast. Inevitably, it would seem, one cannot stand here and not imagine the scene 102 years earlier when the world's largest liner set off to begin its maiden voyage from Southampton, one which would end off Newfoundland at the bottom of the Atlantic.

Three ferries loading, the nearest being the Sealink *Lagan Bridge*, at Belfast Docks in 1980.

The White Star *Nomadic* in front of the *Titanic* exhibition in Belfast. One of the most remarkable survivors of the *Titanic* story is the *Nomadic*, which was the very last ship to sport the famous yellow and black White Star funnel. The *Nomadic* was built alongside the liner at Harland and Wolff in 1912 and ferried 274 passengers at Cherbourg out to the *Titanic*. The *Nomadic* continued to be based there until 1940, when it escaped to serve with the Royal Navy. In 1945, it resumed its work at Cherbourg, serving the Cunard Queens until 1968. In that year, it became a floating restaurant on the Seine in Paris. In 1997, it appeared briefly in the film, *Titanic*. Redundant by 2002, with its history largely forgotten, it was nearly scrapped. Floated back down the Seine, losing most of its upperworks in the process, money was raised to bring it back to Belfast where Harland and Wolff rebuilt it to its 1912 condition, as seen here in the dock where it had been constructed. To sit where the *Titanic* passengers did is a very strange, disturbing experience.

Above: There is now a *Titanic* station in Belfast and here, passing through it in 2014, is a former 80 Class DEMU converted to a Sandite unit, with power car No 8090 bringing up the rear.

Right: A regular and highly enjoyable experience is the Santa Specials that the Railway Preservation Society runs out of Belfast each Christmas. Here, No 85 *Merlin* is preparing to leave, complete with Santa, for Whitehead.

Left: The interior of a Santa Special carriage No 68, a Midland Railway side corridor composite dating from 1922 and transferred to the NCC to compensate for losses in air raids on Belfast during the war.

Below: York Road was the NCC terminus in Belfast. It was badly damaged in the Blitz but survived and here, in the sidings on the approach in 1969, is an MP diesel railcar set. MP stood for multi-purpose, but it might well have meant 'most peculiar', for did you ever see such a variety of carriages formed into one self-propelled set? The oldest, with its ornate, panelled wooden bodies goes back to pre-grouping days; some are non-corridor; one relatively modern, with open layout. I travelled in one such train, from Derry to Belfast, in 1961 – most interesting!

A remarkable and unique survivor is this SLNCR 0-6-4T *Lough Erne*, shunting at York Road in 1969. It and its companion, which date from 1949, were the very last steam locomotives built for service on the standard gauge in Ireland. The wheel arrangement is unusual, but it suited SL&NCR purposes, and the company ordered an updated version of their standard examples from Beyer Peacock. When SL&NCR closed down in 1957, the Ulster Transport Authority found work for it in Belfast, and it eventually passed into preservation with the RPSI.

Great Victoria Street in 1969. This was GNR's terminus in Belfast City Centre, opened in 1839 by the Ulster Railway and known simply as 'Belfast' for the logical reason that there was no other. Rebuilt in 1848, it was always a rather gloomy affair. For all that, it seemed a remarkably retrograde step to close it in April 1976, on the pretext that there was now an alternative in Belfast Central – even though it was not at all central. Wiser counsels triumphed on 30 September 1995, when a new Great Victoria Street opened.

A WT 2-6-4T at York Road in 1969. The last operational steam locomotives employed on normal main line duties within the British Isles, these handsome, workmanlike and efficient locomotives have ensured themselves a special place in railway history.

By 1969, the breaking up of the WTs had begun and one is seen here at York Road undergoing the scrapman's attentions. In the background are some of the wagons used on the spoil trains in the building of the M2 motorway, which kept the last of the WTs employed until 1970.

New Great Victoria Street after its re-opening in 1995. On the right is a Castle Class railcar dating from 1987 and on the left an 80 Class railcar of 1974–78, both built by British Rail Engineering Ltd (BREL). Today, Great Victoria Street has outgrown itself and there are serious proposals to replace it by something bigger and better.

Belfast Central station in 1985. The trouble with its name was that it was not very central, and this was eventually recognised in 2018 when, following a good deal of refurbishment, it became Lanyon Place. In the background is a 70 Class DEMU.

Above left: In 1965, the single-track bridge over the River Lagan, known as the 'Shaky Bridge' for obvious reasons, was removed, cutting off the Bangor line from the rest of the network. It was realised this was a step, or rather a bridge, too far, and a double track one with a pedestrian walk away alongside was erected in 1976, enabling the entire rail network in and around Belfast to be upgraded. A modern NIR CAF class railcar is seen crossing it.

Above right: Over the years, a number of preserved steam locomotives have been employed on the Portrush Flyer. Here is the little GS&WR 0-6-0 No 186, panting somewhat on arrival at Belfast Central after its exertions. Perhaps its admirers are wondering if a pat on its boiler would not go amiss.

Right: On that first journey out of Great Victoria Street to Dublin in 1961, my train of former GNR carriages, many of them dating back to the 1920s, was hauled by one of the UTA WT 2-6-4Ts, several of which were transferred from the NCC section. Here, in preservation days, WT No 4 is calling at Lisburn with its train of CIÉ 1963-vintage Craven carriages.

Antrim in August 1985. The line straight ahead is the NCC one to York Road by way of Ballyclare, whilst the one swinging to the right is the GNR route by way of Knockmore Junction and Lisburn to Belfast Great Victoria Street, which is the one *Slieve Gullion* is about to take. Both are still in existence, although it is many years since the GNR line saw regular traffic.

Above: Up and down Enterprise Expresses pass close to the border between Northern Ireland and the Republic on a misty December morning.

Left: Set in the delightful border country of County Down, this bridge was, and is, a perfect vantage point from which to watch the trains pass underneath. However, there was a time when it was best not to linger.

The remains of B201 at Dundalk, having been hauled back from the vicinity of the border where it had been blown up by IRA members whilst working a freight train from Dundalk to Derry on 15 August 1973. On this occasion, no one was killed or injured. There are those who have never quite understood why an organisation dedicated to bringing the 26 and 6 Counties together thought it a good idea to blow up the railway line that does just that.

In 1970, NIR decided to upgrade the Enterprise and ordered a set of modified BR Mark IIB carriages and three 1,350hp diesel-electric locomotives built at BREL's Doncaster Works, partly by Hunslet, a name once associated with the Irish narrow gauge. When the complete eight-coach train was required, there was a locomotive at each end; at quieter times one sufficed, either pulling or pushing. Here, the southbound train is climbing towards the border.

201 Class 3,200hp Co-Co No 228 of 1995, seen just south of the border with the Belfast-bound Enterprise in 2006. Thirty-four of these very powerful locomotives were delivered from GM in 1994–95, chiefly to work the principal passenger traffic between Dublin and Cork, and Dublin and Belfast.

Above: The Enterprise crosses Craigmore Viaduct (also known as Bessbrook Viaduct) in August 2006. Designed by Sir John O'Neill and brought into use in 1852, this 18-arch, 126ft-high viaduct enabled the line between Dublin and Belfast to be completed. It is both the highest and longest viaduct in Ireland. Through one of its arches the Bessbrook and Newry narrow-gauge electric tramway used to pass.

Left: The tramway closed in January 1948, but one of the cars has survived and here it is being restored at Whitehead.

Below left: The Enterprise must be one of the very few railway services that crosses an international border that is also used regularly as school transport. Here, in 2014, children who have boarded at Drogheda are alighting at Dundalk.

Below right: Dundalk was not only where GNR locomotives were built and repaired but also where they went to die, and here, on 7 September 1961, is V Class Compound No 85 *Merlin*. Sitting amongst a forlorn collection of withdrawn GNR locomotives and tenders, it was, as I recorded at the time, 'the last one, awaiting scrapping'. However, this was not the case, as I discovered later, as *Merlin*, which was performing the odd, not very demanding duty and had been set aside for preservation, was eventually restored to working order by Harland and Woolf.

Right: A damp Hunslet No 101 departs Dundalk for Dublin with the Enterprise, circa 1977.

Below: Dundalk is quite certainly the finest example of GNR architectural style surviving today, and, in modern times, this has been recognised by the careful and sensitive way it has simultaneously been restored and adapted to serve the 21st century.

Dundalk in 2016, with No 29103 arriving on a stopping service from Dublin. It is passing over what used to be the crossover of the line from Greenore; beyond, on the left, was the running shed, whilst the red brick building beside the train was the general store. Dundalk was, in the same was as Crewe, Swindon and Derby for example, a railway town, once employing more than 1,100 men and one or two women. Its closure in September 1958 added considerably to the unemployment statistics of the town.

Above: Drogheda was, and is, the junction for the branch to Navan. Although long closed to passenger traffic, the zinc trains to Dublin Port come this way and here, taking a rest in 2004, are three GMs.

Left: Drogheda in 2003, looking south. On the right is the Belfast-bound Enterprise, on the left a 29000 railcar, whilst approaching the camera are two Irish Rail employees heading for the railcar depot.

Above: At Drogheda station, looking north, with the depot on the right. All its residents would seem to be out on business, apart from a glimpse of one railcar in original black and orange livery.

Left: Kilmessan Junction signal box, which has now been converted into the bridal suite of the hotel on the site of the former station. The station, on the line from Clonsilla to Navan, was opened by the Dublin and Meath Railway in 1862, became the junction for the Athboy branch in 1864, and was absorbed by the MGWR in 1869. Passenger traffic ended in 1947, goods traffic in 1963.

Clonsilla, seen here in September 1995, on the former MGWR main line to the west.

Above left: In September 2010, part of the Navan branch was reopened from Clonsilla as far as M3 Parkway to cater for the growing suburban traffic to and from Dublin city. Here, a train from M3 Parkway is about to set off from Clonsilla for Dublin Docklands in October 2012.

Above right: Butlins opened a holiday camp at Mosney in 1948, which was served by its own station – well, a platform on a loop off the main Belfast to Dublin line. It was immensely popular for decades, with accommodation for 2,800 campers but, eventually, affordable foreign holidays brought about its closure.

Right: Balbriggan possesses a beautiful setting right beside the Irish Sea and was popular originally with day trippers and nowadays with Dublin commuters, but it had a wholly inadequate station when this picture was taken in the 1980s.

Left: Further down the line, towards Dublin Donabate, seen in 1973, was a far more substantial building, proudly displaying its name and dating from 1844. Irish Rail did its customers no favours when it closed the toilets in 2015.

Below: The normal flight path for airliners coming into Dublin from the UK brings them in low over Howth, as in this picture. Howth station is on the extreme top right-hand edge of the harbour. A Holyhead ferry is seen heading out from Dublin port across Dublin Bay.

A few seconds more, and looking from the opposite side of the aircraft, we find ourselves over Malahide, with the Dublin to Belfast main line cutting across the lower part of the picture and then swinging to the right and heading out over the causeway and on to the north.

Above: The Enterprise speeds across the causeway at Malahide. Malahide is a most desirable north-side residential and boating area, the fastest train to Connolly taking a mere 14 minutes.

Right: A GM approaches Dundalk across the causeway with a stopping train for Connolly in April 1991.

Left: If Dundalk is the finest example of a surviving GNR station, Malahide, seen here in April 1991, is the best smaller scale one, much cared for by the community. This is the work of William Henry Mills, the GNR's chief civil engineer.

Below: East- and west-bound ferries passing Howth Head in 2013.

GNR constructed a tramline to the summit of the Hill of Howth from Sutton, one of two intermediate stations between Howth Junction and Howth, in June 1901. Five miles long, it did great business in the summer but lost money the rest of the year. It was closed by CIÉ at the end of May 1959, just before the season began. There were those who suspected that, if it had lasted any longer, the 'head of steam' building up to retain it as a tourist attraction would have proved irresistible. Recently, there have been serious suggestions concerning its revival. (Neil Sparks)

Right: A scene in the National Transport Museum at Howth, with Hill of Howth tram No 9 and Dublin tram No 253. Four Hill of Howth trams have been preserved in Ireland, England and the US. No 9, heavily vandalised, has been painstakingly restored, whilst No 253 has had a somewhat surprising afterlife. Built in 1928, it worked until the very end of the first Dublin tram system in July 1949, then passed to St Joseph's Convent, Dun Laoghaire, where the nuns used it as temporary accommodation. It then moved into preservation, where it was restored by FAS in their workshops at Broombridge.

Below: GNR operated a large fleet of buses and coaches on both sides of the border. Not content with buying from the UK, it built up a substantial fleet of single deckers that it manufactured at Dundalk, fitting them with Gardner engines. This is No 390, of 1951, which has 33 very comfortable seats that enabled it to be used for touring as well as stage carriage services. It is quite famous, a film star no less, having appeared in a number of productions, sometimes in disguise, although never fooling those who know its true identity.

Irish Railways: The Last 60 Years

Sutton, 2009. The depot and power station that once served the tram system are still in place.

Howth Junction in December 1979. Despite the palm tree, the setting, then on the edge of the Dublin suburbs and made famous in the writings of Roddy Doyle, could never be described as exotic. The guard is about to give the right away to his GM-hauled, Connolly-bound stopping train.

At the end of the 1960s, a rake of GS&WR vintage carriages was formed to provide extra capacity for rush hour workings and holiday times along the coast between Bray, Dublin city centre, and Howth. The complement was always changing, as tired vehicles were relieved of their duties and sent for scrap; some of the earliest were arc roofed, the majority non-corridor. Here, the train is heading past Killester on its way to Howth one Saturday afternoon in August 1969.

In 1952–54, CIÉ introduced a fleet of 60 Park Royal-bodied AEC engine railcars, very similar to those already working on GNR. Initially, they were used on long-distance work, but when replaced by GM-hauled trains, they gravitated to suburban duties in the Dublin area. The standard format was a power car at each end with two intermediate carriages. The power available was hardly excessive, but on the flat terrain around Dublin this was not an issue. No 2642 is passing the railcar depot at Fairview, on the edge of Dublin Bay, in 1971, the two intermediate carriages being high-capacity Park Royals.

Right: North Wall was, for a long time, the busiest freight depot in Ireland. Jointly worked by GS&WR, MGWR, GNR and the English LNWR, it was a hive of activity 24/7. Here, in 1975, GM B169 climbs away towards East Wall and the Dublin–Belfast main line. Note the cranes and the forest of TV aerials in the background reaching, if not for the sky, then certainly high enough to pick up signals from either Northern Ireland or Wales.

Below: Re-engined A41R is getting a grip on a lengthy freight bound for the west in the summer of 1970, passing under the line into Connolly. It is running alongside the Royal Canal and will continue to do so for many miles, as far as Mullingar.

One of 12 Sulzer-engined 960hp A1A-A1A locomotives, built by the Birmingham Railway Carriage & Wagon Company in 1956, has charge of a short train of tankers approaching the Granaries yard at North Wall in August in 1977, passing an 001 Class in charge of a freightliner. No 106 was the last active member of its class. One is preserved by the Irish Traction Group.

There was a time when CIÉ had considerable need of shunting locomotives, the most numerous in the diesel era being the Maybach-engined, Inchicore-built E Class, dating from 1955 to 1961. In this November 1973 picture, E413 is engaged in sorting out a very mixed collection of mostly wooden-bodied, and, in some cases, wooden-framed wagons, including the inevitable cattle truck, beside the Royal Canal.

A busy scene at North Wall in August 1996. For decades, the Bellferry container trains were a distinctive feature on the Irish rail network. Here, one is arriving at North Wall from Waterford, the Bellferry's base. Sadly, it is a sight that would be gone forever within a year, with the firm going into liquidation in 1997. However, container trains still serve Dublin, Ballina, Waterford (Belview Port on the River Suir, east of the city), as well as transporting timber from Ballina and Westport. Wikipedia accurately describes it as a 'National rail link running through the port'.

Above: North Wall yards are a mere shadow of what they once were, such is the decline in rail freight in Ireland. A sad scene of frosty dereliction in December 2009, watched over by St Joseph's Roman Catholic Church.

Right: However, one of two traffics that still flourishes is that of zinc. Trains run twice a day from Navan, site of the largest zinc mines in Europe, by way of Drogheda and East Wall Junction. Here, in April 2017, the train is leaving the North Wall yards and is entering Dublin Port territory.

In 2004–05, Irish Rail invested in a fleet of carriages built in Spain by CAF, known as Mark 4s, designed to work between Dublin and Cork pulled or pushed by 201 Class locomotives. On a wet afternoon, they are being unloaded at North Wall and placed onto the tracks, ready to be worked past what was once GS&WR's main freight depot and up to Inchicore before entering service.

With the ever-expanding Dublin suburbs, and the traffic this generated in the early 2000s, Connolly found itself unable to cope. To relieve the pressure, a service began using a new terminus at Docklands, near the site of the container terminal in the former MGWR yard. This was opened by Taoiseach (Prime Minister) Bertie Ahern on 12 March 2007. A 29000 Class railcar from Maynooth approaches Docklands and passes under other 29000 units about to enter Connolly.

Left: Amiens Street on 8 September 1959. GNR UG Class 0-6-0 No 81 of 1937 departs with a stopping train composed of GNR wooden-bodied carriages for Drogheda.

Below: A sight to gladden any steam enthusiast on this September afternoon in 1959 is the 18.25 express to Belfast, pulling out of Amiens Street and hauled by one of the magnificent VS Class 4-4-0s of GNR, still, although owned by the UTA, in its nicely polished sky-blue livery. This was one of five Beyer Peacock-built, Dundalk-designed, three-cylinder simple versions of the V Class Compounds, which were, almost certainly, the very last 4-4-0s built anywhere in the world.

Around the same time, GNR, flush with money after the huge demands put upon it during the war, ordered five more of the light U Class 4-4-0s. This is No 197, one of the original 1915-vintage members of the class, fitted with a post-war tender of almost pure LMS design, arriving at Amiens Street.

T2 Class 4-4-2T No 67 leaving Amiens Street with a Howth train, composed of modern GNR corridor carriages, 8 September 1959. The 20 T2s, entering service between 1921 and 1930, handled much of the suburban traffic around Belfast and Dublin. No 67 was built in 1924 and withdrawn in 1960. A line of cattle trucks forms the background.

The final railcars ordered by GNR before its demise were British United Transport (BUT) ones with through corridor connections beside the cab, Portsmouth-electric style. Here is a six-car, Belfast-bound train composed of four BUT cars and two ordinary carriages, leaving Connolly in 1973. The semaphore signals remain, but they are redundant with the arms removed, and there are still telegraph poles. Beyond these are the Italianate tower of Connolly station and, beyond that, Liberty Hall, the trade union headquarters and the tallest building in the city centre.

Above left: A four-car railcar set leaving Connolly for Howth, headed by No 2637. The two intermediate carriages are a 10ft 2in-wide Bulleid, and a Park Royal.

Above right: The smiles on the lads' faces in this train at Connolly in August 1971 are deceptive, as they are refugees, burned out of their Roman Catholic homes in Belfast by Protestant terrorists and rescued by the Republic government.

The December 1995 low winter sun highlights the impressive lines of No 210 *River Erne*, one of the 34 201 Class 3,200hp GM Co-Cos delivered in 1994–95, and still the most powerful locomotives on the Irish railway network.

Above left: Various shades and combinations of green have been applied to Irish trains and buses over the years. Here, in April 2018, a very green No 29117, the paintwork barely dry, displays its new image in the bay platform at Connolly.

Above right: In 2007, the 071 Class was given a makeover in a livery designed to focus on its concentration on freight duties, but here in the summer of that year, No 082 *The Institute of Engineers of Ireland* – the only named member of the class – still finds itself on passenger work as it is about to depart from Connolly for Sligo.

Right: Just as the DART electrification seemed inevitable in retrospect, so did the arrival of the Luas tram system in Dublin in 2004, 56 years after the demise of its previous one. One of the many benefits was the direct connection by rail of Heuston and Connolly stations. In 2010, a tram is approaching Busáras, the central bus and coach station, just around the corner from Connolly, with a train crossing Gardiner Street Lower on the approach to Connolly in the distance.

In the late 1980s, Irish Rail introduced a fleet of Mk3 push/pull sets to be used mainly, but not exclusively, on Dublin area suburban work. Seen from the top storey of Liberty Hall, a Greystones-bound train, propelled by a 121 Class, is entering Tara Street, the most central of all Dublin railway stations. Some half a mile further on is Pearse station, and the patch of green away to the right is the lawn of Trinity College.

Pearse station was once the starting point for Sligo trains, and, in 1973, a nicely polished A47R is getting ready to depart.

The setting sun picks out the varying outlines of the carriages and vans of the westbound *Galway Mail* as it passes Glasnevin in August 1978. The flat sides of the van nearest the camera belong to a Dutch van – so called because of its Netherlands design – and the last example of a Dundalk-assembled railway vehicle.

Right: The movement of cattle was still big business for CIÉ in August 1973 when Birmingham Railway Carriage and Wagon Company (BRCWC)/Sulzer B105 was passing Glasnevin on its way to North Wall. At the time, the allotments were being cultivated by CIÉ employees.

Below: A35R has charge of the up *Galway Mail* at Glasnevin Junction in August 1975. The track to the left is the former GS&WR one from Islandbridge, near Heuston.

Above: B114, one of the two pioneer CIÉ Inchicore-built, Sulzer-engined main line diesel-electric locomotives of 1950–51, heads past the long wall of Glasnevin cemetery on its way to North Wall in the summer of 1970.

Left: A train load of Guinness on the loop line at Cabra in 1969. The round tower in the distance marks the grave in Glasnevin Cemetery of Daniel O'Connell. The most famous and largest cemetery in Ireland, it is the last resting place of the bodies of many famous Irish men and women and even more ordinary citizens, many of them victims of the famine of the late 1840s.

Heuston station. Kingsbridge, as it was until 1966, is undisputedly the finest piece of railway architecture in the land. However, as I wrote in my *Irish Railways in 1916*, published in 1972, internally 'it is a rather gloomy, low-roofed shed'. Passengers were not allowed in the front door and had to use the side entrance. All that has changed of late, and its refurbishment has resulted in a transformation of the interior. For a long time, it possessed just two platforms, plus one bay, known as 'the military', because it was originally used for troop trains to the military base at the Curragh.

A pair of 121 Class Bo-Bos, once regularly employed on long-distance passenger workings, await the road towards Inchicore from Heuston during the 1970s.

A41R is seen departing Heuston with an interesting collection of empty carriages bound for Inchicore in 1969. First come two ancient GS&WR-built arc-roofed passenger brakes, dating from the first decade of the 20th century, then a 1950s corridor carriage, and bringing up the rear, the State Saloon, which we will see in more detail a little later. Two E Class shunters are going about their business.

Heuston with a wonderful mix of carriages in 1973. On the left is an electric generation van, introduced in 1972 for the BREL Super Trains, whilst to the right are three six-wheelers built before 1900, still finding static employment in departmental service.

Heuston in September 1996. A 201 Class at the head of a train of 40-ton capacity bogie fertiliser wagons dating from 1974 waits for the road.

Welcome the 21st century – if Heuston wanted to really justify its status as Dublin's gateway to the south and west, then money would have to be spent. It was, €170 million to be precise, which brought about a transformation in 2002. With a vastly improved and welcoming concourse, and the number of platforms increased to ten, although there is actually no ninth, the interior is now a fitting match for its magnificent Italianate façade.

Adamstown. Situated 16km from Dublin on the main line to Cork, the town is unique in that it is the only settlement in Ireland in which (practically) its first building was the railway station. I am sure future university generations will use it as an example of study. Planned in 2005 to fill the then seemingly insatiable demand in the days of the Celtic Tiger for yet more and more accommodation within commuting distance of Dublin, one of the very earliest developments was the privately funded station, which opened on 10 April 2007, 14 months after the first houses went on the market. It had the huge misfortune to be struck by the double whammies of the financial crisis of 2008 and then the pandemic of 2020. A report in *The Irish Times* of 1 February 2020 described the station as 'a behemoth (it has five platforms). Bike racks were designed to hold 100 machines, but only a few are in use today'. Sadly, although 10,000 homes were planned, only 1,200 had been constructed when this picture was taken in 2017, many of those unsold. Only 20 minutes from Heuston and 40 from Grand Canal Dock, the possibility for the town to reach its potential, greatly encouraged by the ease of commuting into the city, remains. *The Irish Times* found that those living there spoke well of it, despite many of the promised facilities having not yet arrived.

Inchicore, the principal railway works in Ireland, dates from 1846. Some two miles out of Kingsbridge, it eventually covered 73 acres and provided work for more than 1,000 employees. For many years, a special train, composed of two elderly carriages withdrawn from ordinary service, was provided to carry the workers to and from Kingsbridge/Heuston station. In this 1969 picture, the carriage is No 861, an Edwardian-era, 12-wheel clerestory composite built by the GS&WR for the opening of the Fishguard to Rosslare route. It was retired from the works train in 1972 and sent down the line to Sallins, where condemned carriages were often stored before being removed to Mullingar for breaking up. However, at the very last minute, this magnificent vehicle was rescued by the RPSI, which employed it in its vintage train for many years. It is now undergoing an extensive restoration at Whitehead.

I am pictured next to the State Saloon of 1902 at Inchicore in December 2005. Originally fitted with a clerestory roof, it was rebuilt with its present one in the 1920s, and in 1961 with Commonwealth bogies, which, to quote the late Des Coakham, made it look like a 'dowager in a mini-skirt'. Retired in 1972, it was nearly lost in a fire at Inchicore, but the determined efforts of the RPSI and, in particular Charles Meredith, saw restoration begin at Inchicore in 1995 and, on completion five years later, its launch by Irish President Mary McAleese.

Right: Inside Inchicore Works in 1969, with one of the very disappointing Crossley/Metro Vickers C Class 1,040hp Bo-Bo C220s of 1956–58 being turned into something better with a GM power unit. Alongside, on the left, are railcars being converted into push/pull units to be worked by the re-engined Cs.

Below: The Inchicore 150th anniversary celebrations in the summer of 1996 saw a number of historic items of rolling stock on display, including C Class C231, restored to original CIÉ green livery, as well as A Class A39 in original silver livery but with a GM power unit.

A nine-carriage Cork-bound express accelerates past Inchicore in the summer of 1971, hauled by A22R. It is passing the works train, the carriage nearest the camera being the now-preserved 12-wheel clerestory No 861, the other an arc-roofed GS&WR corridor of the same vintage.

A Cork to Dublin express hauled by two 141 Class GMs, B175 leading, consisting of BREL air-conditioned Super Train carriages, begins its approach to the 1 in 177 descent towards Heuston in 1973. In the distance, the suburbs give way to the countryside, and tall telegraph poles and even taller TV aerials tower over the houses on the other side of the wall beyond the tracks.

Liffey Junction in March 1989. The photographer is standing on the track upon which trains to and from the Broadstone terminus once ran. On the right is the redundant water tower, beyond that the still working signal box controlling trains from Connolly to Mullingar and Sligo and, in the distance, the still more or less intact, but abandoned, Liffey Junction station.

Preserved former DSER 2-6-0 No 461 curves around beside the Royal Canal as it approaches Liffey Junction with an RPSI evening excursion to Mullingar in August 1996.

Above: A Red Line tram and commuter train meet at the rear of the Custom House and close to the Busáras in 2011. The Luas trams are built by Alstom Citadis in La Rochelle, France.

Right: In 2017, the Luas tram system was extended along the length of O'Connell Street, up around the Broadstone and then along the MGWR trackbed, which had not seen passenger traffic since the 1930s, past the site of the now-vanished Liffey Junction and alongside the Irish Rail route to Mullingar to its terminus at Broombridge. This is the view from a tram as it approaches the terminus, the Irish Rail station to the right being in use but not quite complete.

I learned of the existence of the City of Dublin Director's tram just down the hill from the parents-in-law's house in Killiney, in Barnhill Road, Dalkey, but was warned that the owner was a bit of a recluse and did not always welcome enquiries. However, I must have caught him on a good day, or perhaps he was not difficult at all. So here it is, looking absolutely complete, with pole, trucks and accompanying pig.

Not only was I allowed in the yard on that December 1983 afternoon, but I was invited into the interior. It was clearly serving as a somewhat disorganised office, but what was of greater significance was that, beyond the papers, files and so forth, it was in absolute original, untouched, undamaged 1901-era condition; no leaks, no rot of any sort, certainly none that I could see. Negotiations were going on to move it to the National Transport Museum at Howth, but the vandals got to it first, set it alight, and although the substantial remains did get to Howth in 1988, the loss of that near perfect tram is a tragedy.

Above: Sunset at Killiney, in 2009, featuring the headlights of a DART climbing around the cliff edge on its way from Bray to Dublin city with the Sugarloaf Mountain, inland from Bray, on the horizon.

Right: Preserved NCC WT 2-6-4T No 4 on one of its frequent ventures to the Dublin area, storms up the gradient into Killiney station in August 2004 with the RPSI train, the first carriage of GNR origin, the rest 1950s vintage CIÉ.

Dun Laoghaire has claim to be the terminus of the world's first commuter railway, back in its Kingstown days when the line to Dublin opened in 1834. In this 2008 view, two shoppers are heading home alongside Dun Laoghaire station as a southbound DART arrives. I was once informed by a city shopkeeper, who had clearly gotten out of the wrong side of bed that morning, that Dun Laoghaire was far too dangerous a place for respectable citizens, there being an excellent chance of pedestrians either being mugged by a drug addict or squashed by a 4x4. To one such as myself, with more than 50 years acquaintance with the locality, this was news.

Above: For nearly all its distinguished history Kingstown/Dun Laoghaire had been the arrival/departure point of the mail boat, and later, the car ferry to and from Holyhead. In this 1980 view, GM No 175 is pulling out of Carlisle Pier station for Dublin Pearse. Back in those days, as one can see, there was much business for foot passengers, often accompanied by large amounts of luggage.

Left: A car being swung aboard the Holyhead-bound mail boat at Dun Laoghaire in September 1972. Two years earlier, the ferries operated by British Rail had been rebranded Sealink, but were still railway owned. Gradually, the traditional mail boats were replaced by purpose-built car ferries. However, whilst the mail boat still operated, there were occasions when it would find accommodation for a car when, as here, my wife, small son and myself had missed the car ferry and had been taken pity on by the captain of the mail boat who found room for our 1950-vintage Riley RME.

The popularity of Bray as a seaside resort for Dubliners can be judged by this scene, captured in August 1969, as just about every one of the 50-odd doors of this train of wooden-bodied, non-corridor carriages has opened to reveal happy families, fully equipped for a day on the beach, just three minutes away!

The view from Bray Head in 2010, looking down on a six-coach railcar bound for Dublin from Rosslare arriving into Bray.

Above: There was a period in the late 1990s when Irish Rail was short of railcar sets and hired this 80 Class DEMU from NIR to work the shuttle along the spectacular section of line that hugs the edge of the cliffs between Bray and Greystones.

Left: Eventually, in 2000, electrification spread to Greystones and here one of the Japanese Tokyu units, No 8628, which began work in August 2004, is approaching its destination in March 2008.

Further reading from KEY

As Europe's leading transport publisher, we produce a wide range of railway magazines and bookazines.

Visit: shop.keypublishing.com for more details